Ready Set Go!

by **MARK HALE**

STANDARD PUBLISHING
Cincinnati, Ohio

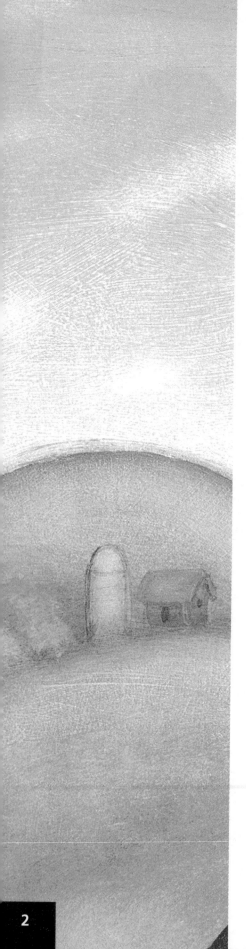

Ready, Set, Go!
© 2000 Mark Hale

Published by Standard Publishing, Cincinnati, Ohio
A division of Standex International Corporation

Credits
Cover design and illustrations by Liz Howe
Interior computer design by Liz Howe and Bob Korth
Acquisitions Editor: Ruth Frederick
Editor: Bruce E. Stoker

07 06 05 04 03 02 01 00   5 4 3 2 1
ISBN 0-7847-1098-8
Printed in the United States of America

About the Author

MARK HALE disciples children through the cutting-edge Bodybuilders Kids Ministry of the Grove City Church of the Nazarene in Grove City, Ohio. He has empowered many others to push the envelope with their ministries through workshops at, among other places, Children's Pastors' Conference. He is also a student, working on his doctorate in education. Mark and his wife Lisa are also training their own three young sons to love and fear the Lord.

Dedication

This book is dedicated to the men who have spurred me on in the faith. For that I am grateful.

My Dads—

Donald Hale, Wayne Reno

My Mentors—

Fred Prince, Donald Joy, Dale VonSeggen

My Pastor—

Bob Huffaker

My Friends—

Steve Combs, Sam Gookin

TABLE OF CONTENTS

INTRODUCTION

READY!

Are you looking for a unique change in the way you accomplish children's ministry at your church? *Ready, Set, Go!* was developed just for you. This book reflects the same teaching techniques used by Jesus himself. If you think about it, Jesus used the outside environment and simple objects to affect his disciples. A stormy sea was just the right tool for Jesus to plunge Peter into a lesson about faith. At Jacob's well, he was able to teach a Samaritan woman the importance of drinking from the spring of eternal life. Another time, while dining in a dingy upper room, Jesus used a water basin and towel to model servanthood and humility.

Ready, Set, Go! provides the backdrop for thirty-five off-site excursions for your kids. Each lesson is scriptural, active, fun, and unique. Sure to break the old classroom routine, *Ready, Set, Go!* promises to be a big hit at your church. But as with any kind of activity, the only way to ensure success is to prepare ahead of time. Each lesson has been broken down into three main sections: READY!—an overview of the lesson and how it relates to the location; SET!—a section to help you prepare for the trip and lesson; and GO!—an outline of the actual lesson with a script to guide you through the activities, stories, interviews, and Scriptures.

SET!

There are a number of different things to keep in mind when you prepare any lesson. By taking your kids off-site, you throw in an endless number of variables—permission slips, medical information, drivers, chaperones, arranging tours, transporting snacks, travel time. The best way to head off any problems and to deal with situations as they occur is to prepare in advance.

Permission Slips

There's no discussion involved here. If you take children away from the place where their parents dropped them off, you need a permission slip. It doesn't matter if the parent is planning to drive or to be a chaperone, the child will still need a permission slip.

Unfortunately, it seems that our society is becoming increasingly litigious, and even churches are beginning to feel the effects. While a "good" lawyer may be able to find some sort of loophole in any legal document with a signature, the signed permission slip is your best legal defense if a parent or guardian decides to sue you or your church.

It's simply a matter of being smart. By requiring a signature on a permission slip that details all the pertinent information about a field trip, you are alerting parents and guardians to all the facts they would need to know. This helps parents to prepare their child properly for the trip, to be prompt in dropping off and picking up their child, and to be aware of any potentially disagreeable destinations or activities. Most important, it forces the parents to become involved.

The sample permission slip provided in this book should be detailed enough to give everyone involved the peace of mind he needs. However, it would be wise to run the form past your church's leadership so they can be aware of what you are distributing and what legal implications it has for the church. They may have suggestions for making the permission slip more useful.

The only reason this permission slip is bundled with the Medical Information Form is to reduce the number of pieces of paper each child must take home, have filled out, and get signed. For that matter you will want to be pro-active about collecting signed permissions slips. While older children can be held responsible for their slips, you may want to check up on younger children who miss the deadline.

Each permission slip should include the following information:

- The child's name
- The parent's or guardian's signature
- The name, address, and phone number of the facility you will visit
- The date of the trip
- The departure and return times
- The purpose of the trip and any unusual activities
- An indication of whether a snack will be provided and what it will be
- An indication of whether any money will be required and how much

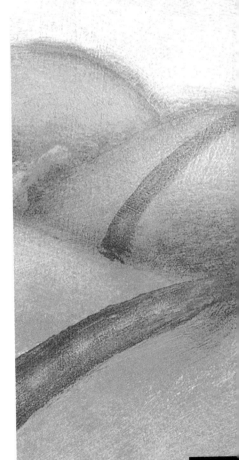

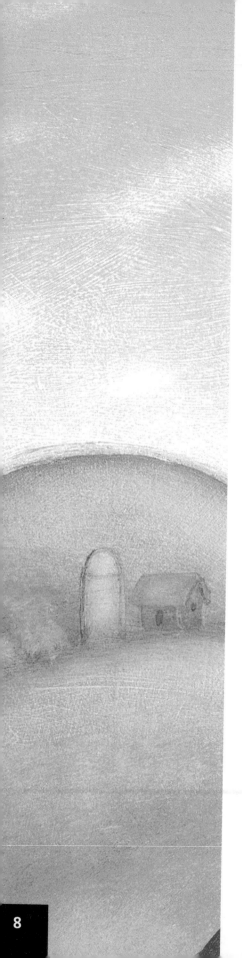

Medical Information Forms

While every medical professional will attest he simply wants to provide the best care for every patient, it is a fact that having complete medical information in-hand will help you get faster, better medical attention. It's not merely a matter of having insurance information; doctors and emergency room personnel run the risk of harming your child if they don't have all the medical facts. That said, though, it's a good idea to have the medical insurance information, as well; a photocopy of the child's insurance card may be a good idea, too.

Each medical information form should include the following information:

- The child's name
- The parent's or guardian's signature
- A statement that the adult representatives of the church are authorized to arrange for emergency transportation to the appropriate facility and to authorize treatment for any emergency medical or dental care.
- The parent's or guardian's address and home and work phone numbers
- The child's medical insurance provider (including the plan name, plan number, and child's identification number)
- A list of all known physical, mental, and medical conditions
- A list of all known allergies, including food allergies
- A list of all past major medical procedures and other medical history

Vehicles, Drivers, and Chaperones

Perhaps one of the toughest things to get ironed out for any field trip is the transportation issue. Even if your church is fortunate enough to have a bus or van to carry all the children and their leaders, there may be other issues to slow you down.

If you are using transportation owned by the church, make sure the church's insurance policy doesn't have restrictions on who is permitted to drive the vehicle. There may be a list of people who are permitted to drive; make sure those people are available or get the right people on the list.

If you have to use personal vehicles, make sure that all the owners and drivers are aware of the destination and who their passengers will be. It would be unfortunate to lose a vehicle at the last minute when one of your drivers suddenly realizes that she is going to have to drive her luxury car up and down a narrow, rocky mountain road and haul children who have just spent the afternoon walking around a pig farm.

You may also have to screen your drivers. While your kids' favorite teacher may offer to drive, it might be wise to have him wait until he has the windshield, headlights, and turn signals replaced in his vintage AMC Gremlin. And it might be a good idea to let the church speed demon wait until after his stint in traffic school.

As for chaperones, that might be a bit easier to deal with. The adults you ask to join you as chaperones don't have to be biblical scholars, police officers, or drill sergeants. They should be adults, both chronologically and socially. While you don't necessarily want to have an adult screaming for the kids to remain silent while they are in the art gallery, you also don't want the 42-year-old church cut-up donning scrubs and delivering babies just to get a laugh.

Regardless of whom you recruit to help with the trips, make sure that everyone is fully informed and fully prepared. Make sure that all of your adults know what their responsibilities are. Make sure all your drivers have directions and a map, and it might be a good idea to have a cellular phone or two among the vehicles just in case there's an emergency or a delay.

Arranging Tours

This is probably the most enjoyable aspect of planning the field trip, but it can also become a real chore. Keep in mind that while I have taken my own youth groups to all of the places in this book, you may not be able to do so. It may take some creative problem solving. For example, what if you don't have a professional ballpark within a reasonable drive? You may have to contact a local university or high school or maybe even the local little league or parks commission. I've tried to offer a number of suggestions for places where you may have some difficulty geting tours, whether because of availability or because of timing, cost, or liability.

Most important, when arranging for tours, is to be professional. While many businesses and organizations have programs and tours as part of their public relations, they are not there simply to accommodate you and your group. Many

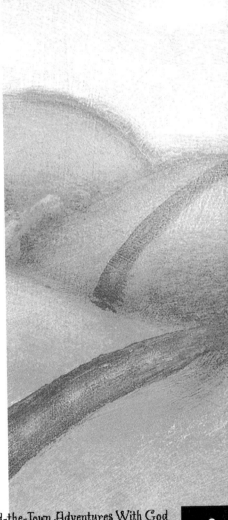

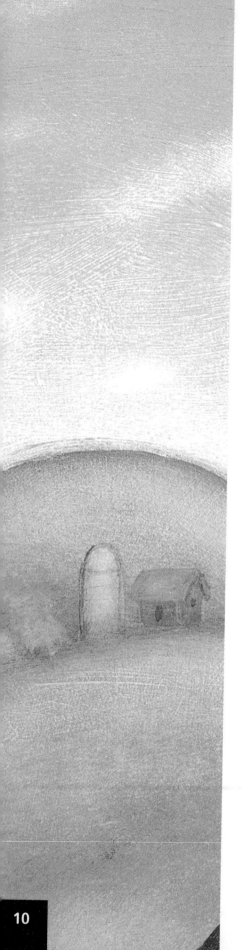

locations may have free give-aways, but some will not. Don't count on them to provide snacks, prizes, or memorabilia. But remember, it doesn't hurt to ask what they can provide; just be sure to do so professionally and with enough lead time for them to accommodate your visit or for you to make other arrangements.

Remember, you are not only arranging for a tour for your children, but you are also representing your church, not to mention Jesus himself, to everyone you meet through these field trips. You should always thank your tour guide or host while planning the trip, as well as during and after it, and be sure to send a thank-you note soon after you return.

Snacks

Snacks can be the bane of children's ministry. There's the question of nutrition, expense, and clean up, not to mention sugar highs and sticky hands and faces. In these lessons, for the most part, I make suggestions for snacks that are appropriate to the lesson, with little thought about these issues. However, you should put some thought into it. You are going to have to decide whether to provide snacks or to allow snacks to be purchased on the trip and whether they are appropriate for the lesson, the location, and the age group.

Perhaps the most important issue you will have to deal with is food allergies. While they are not new, our society is putting more focus on them. Even airlines are cutting nuts from their flights because of the hazards of airborne particles to people with nut allergies. There are all kinds of food allergies, and the only way you are going to avoid problems is to get accurate medical information on all of your kids or to cut out snacks entirely.

GO!

Now that you've made your lists and checked them twice, make sure your lesson is in order; that's the whole reason for going off-site. Evaluate each of the lessons and the activities I have suggested. Depending on the travel time, the size of your group, and the resources at your disposal, you may have to adjust the lesson outline. Most important, though, is to keep the focus intact. It will be lots of fun to visit a Major League Baseball stadium, but if there is no Scripture based lesson involved, it will have no meaning.

Summary

With all these suggestions and cautions in mind, be responsible and safe, but most of all, have fun. Just to make things easier, I've boiled down all the previous advice into the following tips to keep in mind when planning for this program:

1. If discipline is a problem at your church, try using a behavior contract with your children. Basically you will come into agreement with them as to the behavior you expect to see while on *Ready, Set, Go!* trips. A sample form of a contract is included at the end of the introduction.
2. Schedule your trips well in advance. Use the Master Planner as a help to stay organized. A sample form is included at the end of the introduction.
3. For safety, have parents sign a permission slip and medical release form. A sample form is included at the end of the introduction.
4. Have maps ready for all drivers. The "follow the leader" approach almost always backfires as someone loses the caravan.
5. A cellular phone is a must! Bring one in case you break down or if your return trip back to church will be delayed.
6. Break into teams if you have a large group. Assign specific adult leaders to specific groups of children.
7. Prepare Bible references in advance. Instead of having children carry their Bibles to various locations, type out the Bible passage and hand it out to everyone at the site.
8. Have the children dress appropriately for the weather.
9. Always send a thank-you note to the sponsoring location.
10. Brainstorm your own location and lesson ideas. Use *Ready, Set, Go!* as a springboard to your own creativity.

You are now ready. You are now set. It is time to go! It is my prayer that God will take you to places of great adventure and to new spiritual heights when using these lessons.

READY, SET, GO!

MASTER PLANNER

Location _____

Address _____

Contact Person and Phone Number _____

Date of Trip _____ **Approximate Number of Children** _____

Departure Time _____ **Return Time** _____

Leaders Attending _____ _____

_____ _____

Method of Transportation _____

Lesson Name _____

Materials Needed _____ _____

_____ _____

Snacks Provided By _____

Directions to Location

Map to Location

READY, SET, GO!

CHAPERONE/DRIVER REQUEST

Dear Fellow Worker in Christ,

As you've probably heard, the children of the church are participating in an exciting new program called Ready, Set, Go! This series of lessons will take our kids out of the church building and into the world to learn different things from God's Word—we're calling these field trips "around the town adventures with God!"

The success of these lessons largely depends on a lot of detailed preparation and planning. That's where we hope you can help. In order to get our kids to and from each lesson site safely, we need responsible adults who can provide transportation and perhaps assist with the lesson and help keep things running smoothly.

Our next trip will be on _____.

We are going to visit _____.

We will be leaving at _____ and returning at _____.

All I need from you is your commitment to helping our kids learn from God's Word in a unique way. You can do that by driving a few kids to and from the lesson site and by being a chaperone while at the site. If you would like to help with future lessons, whether by driving or in other ways, please let me know.

Thanks in advance for your help!

Sincerely,

READY, SET, GO!

MEDICAL INFORMATION AND PERMISSION SLIP

Child's Name _____ **Date of Birth** _____

Home Address _____

Parent or Guardian's Name _____ **Home Phone Number** _____

Father's Employer _____ **Phone Number** _____

Mother's Employer _____ **Phone Number** _____

Insurance Provider _____ **Policy Number** _____

List of Known Allergies _____

Other Person to Call in Case of Emergency: Name _____ **Phone Number** _____

Child's Physician _____

General Medical History _____

_____

Additional Comments _____

_____

By signing this form, I give permission for my child to attend Ready, Set, Go! I also give consent and authorization for emergency transportation and any medical treatment my child may require in the unlikely event my child be injured while on a field trip during Ready, Set, Go!

_____   _____
Parent/Guardian Signature   Date

READY, SET, GO!

RESPONSIBILITY CONTRACT

Please understand these guidelines are being set forth so as to make Ready, Set, Go! a great ministry for all involved. Because safety is so important for a program of this nature, there will be no tolerance for any unsafe activity. Also, please realize *you* are the reason this program has been developed. The Ready, Set, Go! Leadership Team believes in you and knows we can count on you.

Sincerely,

I promise to make every effort in helping the Ready, Set, Go! Leadership Team make Ready, Set, Go! a fun and meaningful time for all children. I also agree to the following:

1. I will stay with the group at all times.

2. a. While in the bus, van, or car, I will keep all conversation to a low speaking voice so as not to distract the driver. I will not yell.
   b. I will keep my hands and arms inside the vehicle at all times.
   c. I will keep the vehicle clean.
   d. I will not throw anything while in the vehicle.
   e. I will show respect to my Ready, Set, Go! leaders.
   f. I will shine my flashlight only at appropriate times and not while I'm in a vehicle.

3. I will not drink beverages or bring snacks in the vehicle.

4. During the lesson, I will listen, participate, and not disrupt.

5. When asked to settle down, I will *immediately be quiet* and listen for instructions.

6. To ensure the safety of others, I will not roughhouse or horse around during Ready, Set, Go!

Child's Name _____ Date _____

Grade _____ Phone Number _____

BATTING CAGE

Focus: *God can change your direction.*
Scripture: *2 Corinthians 5:17*

READY!

A batting cage is not only a great place to have fun but also to learn a valuable faith lesson. There you can discuss the fact that when someone is converted, their life changes direction. They are no longer running away from God. Instead, they are moving toward God.

SET!

If the batting cage has been closed down for your use, ask to tour the inside area where the baseballs are fed into the pitching machine. Ask the tour guide to explain how the balls are expelled and rocketed toward a batter. Make sure that when you have toured the cage, the children will be able to try their luck at hitting a few balls.

GO!

Visit the batting cages and have the guide demonstrate how the pitching machine works. Let the kids ask any questions they may have. After the tour, have the kids gather near one cage for the object lesson.

After the object lesson, continue with the rest of the lesson.

What Does God Say?

Say: **Do you remember the man in the Bible named Saul? He was a guy who totally changed directions. At first, Saul hated Christians or anyone who followed Jesus. He was known to hunt down those who believed in the Lord and have them imprisoned or even killed. But one day when Saul was travelling on a road to a city called Damascus, Jesus appeared to him in a bright light that blinded him. While he was blind, Saul asked Jesus to forgive him. Jesus did, and he restored Saul's sight. Saul then became a Christian and stopped persecuting Christians. This change of heart was so dramatic that Saul even changed his name to Paul and became one of the greatest missionaries in the world. For the rest of his life, he preached the good news that Jesus can save all people.**

Even when kids become Christians, they, too, will change direction. Soon they will want to stop doing things that are against God's will. Instead, with the help of God's Holy Spirit, they will choose to go God's way.

The next time you watch a ballplayer hit a home run, remember that the ball has changed directions. Also, remember that, with God's help, you can change direction, too.

Wrap Up

Read aloud 2 Corinthians 5:17. Say: **When someone becomes a Christian, he becomes a brand new person. He is not the same any more. A new life has begun.**

Ask your adult helpers or children to share testimonies of how God has turned them around. Close in a circle of prayer.

OBJECT LESSON
Needed: batting helmet, baseball, and bat
Set Up: none
Message: Sometimes it takes a dramatic change of direction to follow Jesus.

Say: **In the batting cage your purpose was to hit the ball. In a real game, your goal is the same. As the ball leaves the pitcher's hand, the object is to follow the ball with your eyes and swing your bat at the very point contact can be made. Some of us are better at this than others. Mark McGwire, Sammy Sosa, Babe Ruth, and Roger Maris have proven themselves to be true home-run hitters.**

Have you ever hit a home run in a little league, church league, or school game? How did you feel when your bat hit the ball? Regardless of how you felt, something amazing happened. The ball, which was whirled in one direction, made contact with the bat and actually stopped in mid-air, then completely changed direction. And before you knew it, you were running the bases with a hit!

GREENHOUSE

MUST SEES
- Seed area
- Hot house
- Fertilizer, manure
- Potting area

SNACK
Dirt pudding (chocolate pudding mixed with gummy worms and crumbled chocolate sandwich cookies)

MUST HAVES
- Healthy potted plant in good, rich soil
- Dead or unhealthy potted plant in rocky, sandy, unfertile looking soil
- Enough small potted plants or seedlings for each child to have one

TO-DO LIST
- Arrange for tour at a greenhouse where the kids will be sure to see all the stages of a plant's growth process.
- Purchase a small potted plant for each child or begin growing some plants from seeds in Styrofoam cups or small milk cartons (begin this well in advance of the trip).

ASSIGNMENT
Give each child a small potted plant. Encourage the children to take the plant home and care for it. Then plan a day, some weeks later, when the children can bring their plants back to church so that all can see the progress.

Focus: *Planting God's Word in the right soil.*
Scripture: *Luke 8:4-15*

READY!

The local greenhouse or garden center is an appropriate place to discuss the parable of the sower. It is important to remember that simply because people hear God's Word does not mean the Word is growing and thriving in the hearts and lives of our children. Through this lesson, your children will begin to realize the truth of God's Word.

SET!

Arrange for your group to tour and experience what happens in a greenhouse. Show them the area where seeds are nurtured into maturity. Look at and touch the different kinds of soils, seeds, and fertilizers. Be sure to instruct your children to use their sense of smell, because there are numerous things giving off unique scents. These could include plants, flowers, mulch, and manure.

GO!

Visit the different areas of a greenhouse to show the different stages of a plant's growth cycle. Have the tour guide explain the importance of caring for plants. Near the end of the tour, do the object lesson.

What Does God Say?

After the object lesson, gather the children together for the rest of the lesson.

Say: **There are many boys and girls in this world who hear about the saving power of Jesus, but for some reason they let the devil steal the truth from their hearts. Others hear God's message and receive it into their lives. They ask Christ to forgive them of their sins. But because they neglect God and do not go to him for spiritual nourishment, their relationship with him withers up and dies. Their roots don't go deep into God.**

Others let the things of this world take the life out of their relationship with Jesus. Sports, money, or friends become so important in their lives that they choke out any room which should have been given to God.

Then there are those who grow when they hear and accept God. Like the good soil, their hearts are ready for God's truth which is the seed. The Bible says that they "retain it" (Luke 8:15, NIV). That means the seed won't fall out and the seedlings won't dry up and die. Eventually that relationship with Jesus will grow into maturity.

Wrap Up

Have the children join hands and make a circle. Spend time praying for each child. Ask God to continue to plant his Word in the hearts and lives of the children. Also, pray that the children will be open and responsive to God's Word.

After you pray, give the kids their assignment.

OBJECT LESSON
Needed: *two potted plants*
Set Up: *One plant should be flowering and healthy. Its soil should look dark, rich, and fertile. The other plant should be dried up and dead. Its soil should look rocky, unhealthy, and unfertile. You may have to actually work at making the soil look this way. Adding pebbles, sand, and clay soil will add to the effect.*
Message: *Tender, fertile soil produces healthy plants. In the same way, tender, fertile hearts will produce lives growing in faith.*
Read Luke 8:4-15.
Say: ***According to God's Word, the Bible, the message of salvation—that God loves everyone and wants to forgive all people of their sins—is much like a seed. It needs to be planted and nurtured so it can grow. But for some folks, that message never really sinks in, and it doesn't grow. It is kind of like this old, dead plant.*** *(Hold up the plant.)* ***What do you think killed this poor little guy?*** *(Wait for answers.)* ***This plant has been watered and placed in the sun so that it could grow. It was sheltered from cold winds and harsh rain. So what happened to it? Why did it die? Take a look at the soil. It does not look very healthy. There are rocks and clay mixed into it. The dirt looks as though it contains no nutrients.***

The funny thing is that when the seed was planted, it sprouted up and looked like it would grow to be a beautiful flower. But because the rocks were so thick and the moisture could not sink deep to the base, the plant died.

Look at this plant. *(Hold up the healthy plant.)* ***It looks as healthy as can be. The leaves are green. The flower has bloomed. There are no dried-up roots or petals. Nothing is dying. So why is the plant doing so well?***

Look at its soil. It appears to be fertile. The dirt is dark and full of nutrients. There are no rocks or clay to choke out the roots. In fact, the roots are able to reach down into this pot and find the nourishment that helps the plant grow. The seed planted in this pot grew because it fell into good soil.

LAUNDROMAT

Focus: *God can make you clean.*
Scripture: *Isaiah 1:18*

READY!

The laundromat is a great place to discuss how God's grace and love can set us free and cleanse us from the dirt of sin.

Many kids feel guilty for the sins they have committed, whether it be cheating on a test, gossiping, or disobeying their parents. It seems as though today's youth, even those in the church, do not understand that when God forgives our sins, he removes the stain or blemish which would otherwise separate us from him.

Included in this lesson is the story "Ragman" by Walter Wangerin, Jr. It is a treasure for those who wish to explain how God can launder our sin-stained rags and make them clean and new.

SET!

Arrange for your group to go to the local laundromat. You may want to check with a local hospital or an institution, such as a prison or a school, that might have a laundry or laundry service. Such an institution may have huge washers and dryers that may be more impressive than the typical coin-fed ones at a laundromat. Your community might also have a laundry that also does dry cleaning and ironing.

GO!

Visit the laundromat. Have your children simply observe the washers and dryers already in use. Have them feel the dryers and notice the heat which they exert. Have them smell the sweet scent of laundry detergent being used to clean the clothes. Begin the T-shirt object lesson. While the shirt is being washed, read "Ragman" by Walter Wangerin, Jr.

Story Time—"Ragman"

I saw a strange sight. I stumbled upon a story most strange, like nothing my life, my street sense, my sly tongue had ever prepared me for.

Hush, child. Hush, now, and I will tell it to you.

Even before the dawn one Friday morning I noticed a young man, handsome and strong, walking the alleys of our City. He was pulling an old cart filled with clothes both bright and new, and he was calling in a clear, tenor voice: "Rags!" Ah, the air was foul and the first light filthy to be crossed by such sweet music.

"Rags! New rags for old! I take your tired rags! Rags!"

"Now, this is a wonder," I thought to myself, for the man stood six-feet-four, and his arms were like tree limbs, hard and muscular, and his eyes flashed intelligence. Could he find no better job than this, to be a ragman in the inner city?

I followed him. My curiosity drove me. And I wasn't disappointed.

Soon the Ragman saw a woman sitting on her back porch. She was sobbing into a handkerchief, sighing, and shedding a thousand tears. Her knees and elbows made a sad X. Her shoulders shook. Her heart was breaking.

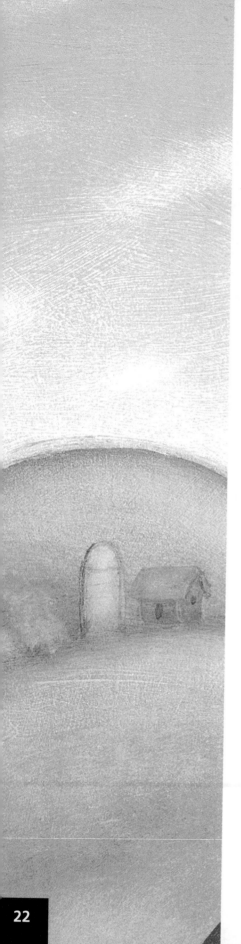

The Ragman stopped his cart. Quietly, he walked to the woman, stepping round tin cans, dead toys, and Pampers.

"Give me your rag," he said so gently, "and I'll give you another."

He slipped the handkerchief from her eyes. She looked up, and he laid across her palm a linen cloth so clean and new that it shined. She blinked from the gift to the giver.

Then, as he began to pull his cart again, the Ragman did a strange thing: he put her stained handkerchief to his own face; and then *he* began to weep, to sob as grievously as she had done, his shoulders shaking. Yet she was left without a tear.

"This *is* a wonder," I breathed to myself, and I followed the sobbing Ragman like a child who cannot turn away from mystery.

"Rags! Rags! New rags for old!"

In a little while, when the sky showed grey behind the rooftops and I could see the shredded curtains hanging out black windows, the Ragman came upon a girl whose head was wrapped in a bandage, whose eyes were empty. Blood soaked her bandage. A single line of blood ran down her cheek.

Now the tall Ragman looked upon this child with pity, and he drew a lovely yellow bonnet from his cart.

"Give me your rag," he said, tracing his own line on her cheek, "and I'll give you mine."

The child could only gaze at him while he loosened the bandage, removed it, and tied it to his own head. The bonnet he set on hers. And I gasped at what I saw: for with the bandage went the wound! Against his brow it ran darker, more substantial blood—his own.

"Rags! Rags! I take old rags!" cried the sobbing, bleeding, strong, intelligent Ragman.

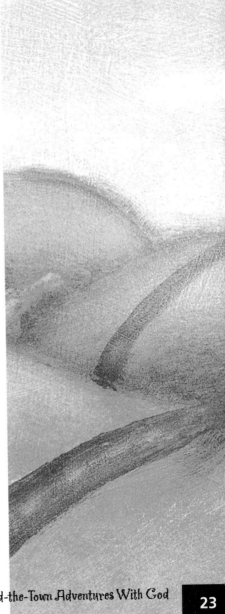

The sun hurt both the sky, now, and my eyes; the Ragman seemed more and more to hurry.

"Are you going to work?" he asked a man who leaned against a telephone pole. The man shook his head.

The Ragman pressed him: "Do you have a job?"

"Are you crazy?" sneered the other. He pulled away from the pole, revealing the right sleeve of his jacket—flat, the cuff stuffed into the pocket. He had no arm.

"So," said the Ragman. "Give me your jacket, and I'll give you mine."

Such quiet authority in his voice!

The one-armed man took off his jacket. So did the Ragman—and I trembled at what I saw: for the Ragman's arm stayed in its sleeve, and when the other put it on he had two good arms, thick as tree limbs; but the Ragman had only one.

"Go to work," he said.

After that he found a drunk, lying unconscious beneath an army blanket, an old man, hunched, wizened, and sick. He took the blanket and wrapped it round himself, but for the drunk he left new clothes.

And now I had to run to keep up with the Ragman. Though he was weeping uncontrollably, and bleeding freely at the forehead, pulling his cart with one arm, stumbling for drunkenness, falling again and again, exhausted, old, old, and sick, yet he went with terrible speed. On spider's legs he skittered through the alleys of the City, this mile and the next, until he came to its limits, and then he rushed beyond.

I wept to see the change in this man. I hurt to see his sorrow. And yet I needed to see where he was going in such haste, perhaps to know what drove him so.

The little old Ragman—he came to a landfill. He came to the garbage pits. And then I wanted to help him in what he did, but I hung back, hiding. He

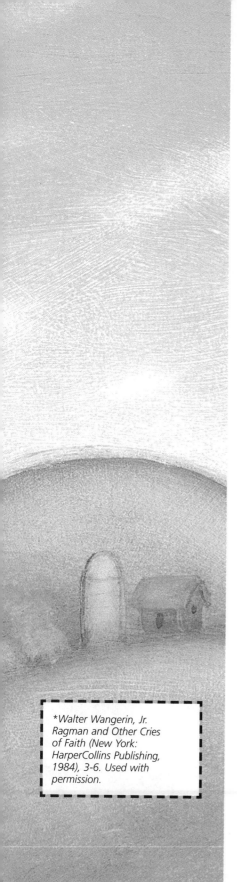

*Walter Wangerin, Jr.
Ragman and Other Cries
of Faith (New York:
HarperCollins Publishing,
1984), 3-6. Used with
permission.

climbed a hill. With tormented labor he cleared a little space on that hill. Then he sighed. He lay down. He pillowed his head on a handkerchief and a jacket. He covered his bones with an army blanket. And he died.

Oh, how I cried to witness that death! I slumped in a junked car and wailed and mourned as one who has no hope—because I had come to love the Ragman. Every other face had faded in the wonder of this man, and I cherished him; but he died. I sobbed myself to sleep.

I did not know—how could I know?—that I slept through Friday night and Saturday and its night, too.

But then, on Sunday morning, I was wakened by a violence.

Light—pure, hard, demanding light—slammed against my sour face, and I blinked, and I looked, and I saw the last and the first wonder of all. There was the Ragman, folding the blanket most carefully, a scar on his forehead, but alive! And besides that, healthy! There was no sign of sorrow nor of age, and all the rags that he had gathered shined for cleanliness.

Well, then I lowered my head and, trembling for all that I had seen, I myself walked up to the Ragman. I told him my name with shame, for I was a sorry figure next to him. Then I took off all my clothes in that place, and I said to him with dear yearning in my voice: "Dress me."

He dressed me. My Lord, he put new rags on me, and I am a wonder beside him. The Ragman, the Ragman, the Christ!

After reading the story, ask these questions of your group of children.

1. How did the Ragman remove the sins and problems of those whom he met? (He exchanged their dirty

rags—the woman's handkerchief, the girl's bandage, the angry man's jacket, and the drunk's blanket—with shiny, new articles.)

2. **What happened to the people who gave the Ragman their dirty rags?** (They were healed and made whole.)

3. **What happened to the Ragman at the garbage dump?** (He died, and three days later he rose again.)

4. **Why did the Ragman die?** (Because he took upon himself the desolate condition of those he met. He did this because he loved them.)

5. **How were the dirty rags like sin?** (They represented how man is corrupted and in need of help. The people in the story were without hope. People in today's world who are caught up in sin also feel hopeless.)

6. **How is the Ragman like Jesus?** (Jesus took the punishment for our sins by dying on the cross. Like the Ragman, for those who believe, he gives them a new spiritual life.)

When you finish the questions, finish the T-Shirt object lesson.

Wrap Up

Say: **Just as we couldn't remove the stains on our dirty shirt, we also cannot remove the stain or consequences of our sin. That's why Jesus came and died. He took our punishment so that we would not be held responsible. He alone became the cleanser of our dirty hearts.**

In Isaiah 1:18, God says, "Your sins are red like deep red cloth. But they can be as white as snow. Your sins are bright red. But you can be white like wool" (ICB).

End by allowing your chaperones and kids to testify to God's saving love at work in their lives. Close in a circle of prayer.

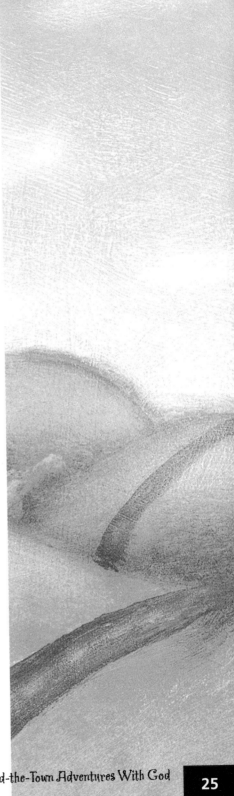

PIG FARM

Focus: *Stay close to God.*
Scripture: *Luke 15:11-32*

READY!

A pig farm may be the smelliest of all the *Ready, Set, Go!* locations. For those who know the story of the prodigal son, the pig farm represents the reward for disobedience. Anyone who has turned away from a life with Christ will eventually realize just how much it really "stinks." Use this lesson to illustrate how important it is to stay close to God and—perhaps more important—how it is possible to return to God even when we run away from him.

SET!

Contact a local pig farm and arrange to take a tour. Make sure the kids will be able to see the pigs' food, their feeding area or trough, their pens, and the barnyard.

Prior to your lesson, purchase fake pig noses for each child at an area costume or novelty store. Allow your children to wear the noses only during the skit.

GO!

See how pigs live, eat, and sleep. Ask to see their food, pen, and trough. Be sure the person showing you the farm can answer questions provided by the children. You may also use these questions:

1. How much does the average pig weigh?

2. How old do pigs get?

3. Are pigs smart or dumb animals?

4. What happens to the pigs once they leave the farm?

5. Why are they so messy?

What Does God Say?

For the next portion of the lesson, gather your children in an area where there is room to act out a skit. You may want to find a location up-wind from the pens. Tell the children to wear the pig noses for the duration of the skit. Assign them to "oink" or squeal whenever they hear the word *pig* in the story. (You may wish to practice this procedure prior to reading the story.)

There once was a man who had two sons he loved very much. In fact, he always gave his sons bear hugs.

One day, the younger son said to his dad, "Hey, Pop, why not let me have some of your life savings?" So the dad divided up his money and gave half to his younger son. Not long after that, the younger son took all of his money, gave his dad a bear hug, and set off for a distant country. He walked and walked and walked.

As soon as he landed in the foreign country, he spent all of his money. He gave it away to everyone who promised him fun. After he had spent all his money, he turned his pockets inside-out looking for more. When he realized there was no more money, he began to pout. Then he started to sob, and eventually he was bawling like a baby—he even started sucking his thumb.

Soon there was a famine in the land, and the younger brother became hungry. His stomach growled like a ferocious lion! He began looking for a job and eventually found work at a pig farm. Like most Jews, the younger brother hated pigs. He despised pigs! But

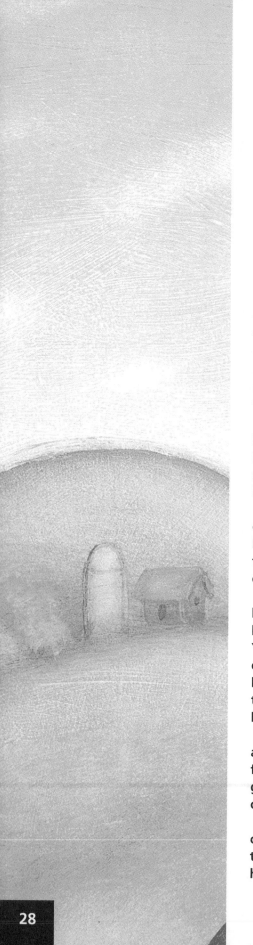

taking care of pigs was his only choice. He was so hungry and his stomach growled so loudly that he soon longed to get on his hands and knees and eat the stuff that pigs eat. And so the younger son did just that.

Eventually, after eating a lot of pig food, he came to his senses—almost as though he were knocked on the head. He said, "Man, if I had just stayed at home, I'd have plenty to eat. Even my father's servants eat better than these pigs!" So, he decided he would walk back to his dad's home, and there he would ask for forgiveness. He kissed those pigs good-bye forever.

So he walked and walked, skipped, and even walked backwards until he finally reached the hill by his dad's home. But while he was still a long way off, his father got out his binoculars and saw him approaching. He began to jump up and down in excitement.

The father had compassion on his son and skipped out to see him. The son dropped to his knees and kissed his father's feet. He said to his father, "Dad, I'm so sorry that I ran away and wasted your money. Please let me come home. Hire me as one of your servants."

The father was so happy to see his son that he helped his son jump to his feet and gave him a bear hug. He said to his son, "Make you a servant? No way! You're my son, and you are always welcome home, even when you run away." While he was hugging him he held his nose, for his son smelled like a pig. Then he told his servants, "Go get my best clothes and clean my boy up. Then fire up the grill. We're having a party!"

So the servants ran and got their master's best suit and cleaned up the younger son. They put rings on his fingers and shoes on his feet. Then they prepared a great big feast and started the party. There was a lot of dancing and singing.

There was so much noise from the party that the older brother heard it way out in the fields. He thought there was a riot. When he got closer to home, he asked one of the servants what was going on.

The servant told him, "Your brother, who ran away and wasted your father's money, has returned, and your father is throwing a big welcome home party."

The older son got mad. No, he got really mad. I mean he was furious. He was so mad that he wanted to break something. He jumped up and down and screamed.

Hearing the noise, the father went out to his older son and asked what was wrong.

His son said, "That selfish little brat you call a son took your money, ran away and spent it all. Now he's come home and you give him a party? I stayed home and worked like a slave for you, and you wouldn't even let me go get a pizza with my friends. It's not fair!"

The father said, "You're right. Your brother was foolish and ran away, but now he's come home! Why shouldn't I be happy? You stayed by my side through everything. You worked harder than all my servants. Remember, someday, all of this will be yours. But for now, be happy that your lost brother has come home!"

After the skit, have the children remove their pig noses and answer these questions:

1. What was the moral of this story? (It's never too late to be forgiven.)

2. How does this story relate to our spiritual life? (Sometimes people think that having a "good time" is more important than serving God.)

3. What was the son's big mistake? (Leaving in the first place.)

4. Have you ever been tempted to not go to church so that you could go and do your own thing? How do you think God feels about that? (It makes Him feel sad.)

Wrap Up
Close by allowing the kids to pray for anyone they know who has chosen to walk away from God.

DOG POUND

MUST SEES
- Holding area
- Cleaning area
- Operating room
- Pens

SNACK
Vanilla wafers (they remind a person of dog biscuits)

Focus: *Follow the Master.*
Scripture: *Matthew 18:12-14*

READY!

The local humane society, animal shelter, or dog pound is just the right environment to discuss the heartache and dangers of being lost. Many of the children in your group will have experienced one of their pets running away and becoming lost. The pain for the child is nearly unbearable.

Being lost is no fun for the dogs, either. Often these lost or abandoned pets end up in the dog pound or animal shelter. There they are placed in cages while they wait for their masters to come and retrieve them.

In the same way, running away from God can be traumatic. Many people who are lost don't know that Jesus wants to be their guide. Others are quick to respond to the Master's call. Whatever the case, God's Word has a lot to say about being lost.

MUST HAVES
- A variety of candles (short, tall, skinny, fat)

TO-DO LIST
- Make sure the kids will be able to bond with the dogs while they are at the pound.
- Collect a variety of candles for the story.

SET!

Make arrangements to tour a local dog pound or animal shelter. Ask that the director or resident veterinarian conduct the tour. At the facility, ask to see the room where the dogs are initially taken when they come off the streets. Ask what process is used to clean and check the dogs. Also, be sure to see the operating room. Finally, ask to see where the dogs are housed. Make sure that the kids will be able to see some of the dogs. See whether it will be possible for the director or veterinarian to bring some of the dogs out of the cages so the kids can pet and play with them.

GO!

Take a tour of the local dog pound or animal shelter. Go through the center as though you are following the path of a lost dog that was taken to the center. Go through the whole process with the tour guide. Be sure to see as many dogs as possible, and try to allow the children to bond with some of the dogs. Perhaps the tour guide will be able to let the kids play with some of the dogs. Ask these questions or any other questions the children may have:

1. **How many dogs are brought to this place every week?**

2. **Are most dogs runaways or do their owners abandon them?**

3. **Do most dogs wear dog tags? How does this help in getting the dog back to its owner?**

4. **What kind of special care is given to the dogs while they are here?**

5. **How long are most dogs here?**

6. **What happens to the dogs that are not picked up?**

Read the story "Captain Candle."

Story Time— "Captain Candle"

Boys and girls, let me start off by asking you how many of you have ever been lost. Some of you have probably been lost in the supermarket or at church or school. Being lost isn't fun.

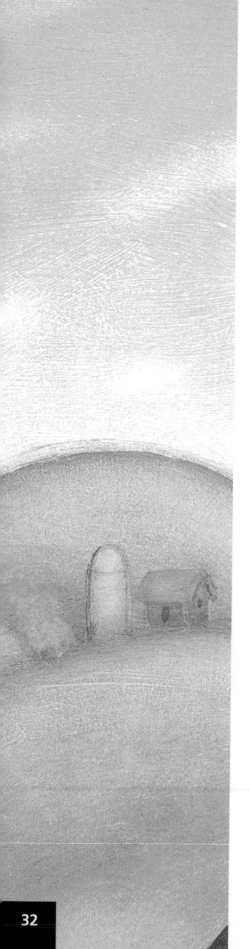

Well, the story I want to tell you takes place in the desert. If you know anything about the desert, you know it is a frightening place. The heat is terrible and there is no one around for miles. What a place to be lost!

Our story begins with the Candle Kids. They are young children just like you, but they are candles. Some are tall like the candles on your dinner table. Others are fat like the kind used around the holidays. Some are the kinds you use to light pumpkins on Halloween. Still others are small, simple birthday candles. The Candle Kids are quite a group and sightseeing in the desert is what they were doing.

As the kids traveled through the desert, they rode in the back of someone's pickup truck. That may not sound like a problem, but it became one when the truck hit a huge pothole and every one of the Candle Kids was thrown clear. They got up as quickly as they could and began to yell, "Hey, come back; wait, wait, come back!" Unfortunately, the truck was long gone.

They walked to the side of the road and some began to panic. Fat Brown who was a large brown candle yelled, "Do you know what this means? We're lost! We're not only lost, we're really, really lost. Then small, little Penny Purple began to cry, "Someone please, please help us."

"What are we going to do?" sobbed the Candle Kids. "Isn't there anyone who can help us? Isn't there anyone who can save us?" You know, boys and girls, it looked pretty hopeless. But then, suddenly without introduction, he appeared. It was . . . Captain Candle.

He was a big, orange, strong-looking candle. And as the Candle Kids looked at him, they thought maybe he could help them. Maybe he knew the way and could be their guide. After the Candle Kids explained their story and had told him everything that had happened, Captain Candle cleared his throat and spoke. "I will be your guide and I will help you. But you will have to follow me. You will have to do exactly what I say."

Off across the desert they began to walk. Step after step and mile after mile. "There's a town ahead," said the captain. "But it's many miles away. Our journey will be dangerous. So stay close to me. If you do, I'll lead you to safety."

They walked for hours. The heat was nearly unbearable. Beads of wax dripped from their brows. "Keep the faith, Candle Kids," said the captain. "We'll make it."

The cliffs and rocks were very dangerous. One wrong step and one would have surely broken an arm or leg or even a wick! But with each step, the Candle Kids drew courage from Captain Candle.

As the group made it to a clearing, Captain Candle showed the kids the canyon they would have to cross. Looks of fear and discouragement swept their faces. They weren't sure they could make it. But Captain Candle told them the same thing he told them at the beginning of their journey. "If you follow me and stay close, doing just as I tell you, I'll lead you to safety."

As the night began to fall, the kids were frightened. "How can we see in the dark? How will we know which way to go?" With that, Captain Candle struck a match and lit the wick on top of his head. "My light will be your guide, kids. Use my light and follow me. I will lead you to safety." The light he shed gave them direction to safety throughout the dark, desert night.

Just as daybreak came, the Candle Kids began to jump up and down. Pointing with their fingers, they said, "Look, look! There's a town in the distance. We are going to be all right. We made it. We are safe."

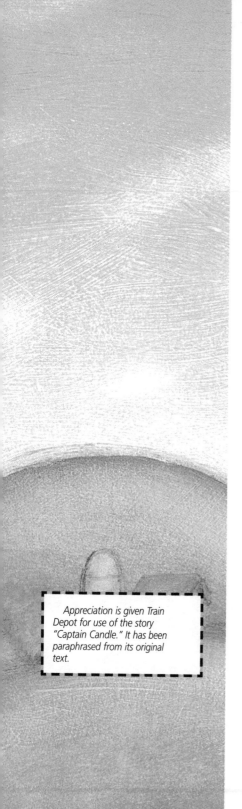

"Wait, where's the captain? Where's he gone?" someone asked. In all the excitement, they had almost forgotten about him. They began to yell, "Captain, Captain, where are you?" Unfortunately, there was no answer. The Candle Kids looked everywhere until finally one of them found the captain. The Candle Kids couldn't believe their eyes and they all began to cry.

The captain had completely melted into a small puddle of wax. He had walked his last mile. He knew that to get the Candle Kids to safety through the night that he would have to keep his light lit even though it would surely melt him away. But he loved those kids so much that he kept it lit anyway. One of the kids spoke up and said, "He gave his life for us. He didn't have to. He didn't have to help us, but he did it, and it cost him everything he had. It cost him his life."

As they watched the last part of flame flicker out, it reminds us of another story – a story of a man named Jesus. You see, he came for those who are lost. And just like Captain Candle, Jesus, too, gave His life. He didn't have to, but He did it because He loved us. He knew that unless He died on the Cross, there would be no way for us to be saved.

What Does God Say?

Read Matthew 18:12-14.

Say: **Obviously, God does not want anyone to be lost. That's why he sent his Son, Jesus, to come and be our guide. If we allow him to be our master, he will keep us safe. He will never abandon us to a place where there is little hope. Instead, he will adopt us into his family and we will be his children.**

Wrap Up

Pray and ask that God would bring home the lost sheep—our friends and family who do not follow God.

TRAIL WITH FOOTBRIDGE

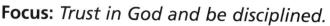

Focus: *Trust in God and be disciplined.*
Scripture: *Matthew 7:13, 14*

MUST SEES
• *Narrow trail*
• *Steep pathway*
• *Footbridge*

SNACK
Trail mix (granola, dried fruit, nuts, pretzels, chocolate candies, etc.)

READY!

Most people have hiked a path through a park or in the mountains or in the country. Many times there are streams, gulleys, or valleys of some sort that need to be crossed. If you've ever had to figure out a way to cross such an obstacle, you can appreciate how helpful a bridge can be. Use this lesson to explain two key biblical truths: that the path to heaven is narrow and that Jesus is the bridge from where we are to heaven.

SET!

Explore your local city parks for a narrow trail which includes along its path a footbridge. Choose a trail that is one-fourth to one-half mile long and loops back to your starting point. If the path has a few other obstacles, such as downed trees or steep or rocky terrain, it will help reinforce the point. If you have someone in your church who can identify wild plants and flowers as well as the different tree species, invite them to come and offer their expertise along the way.

Be sure to remind the kids to dress appropriately; it is especially important to have them wear appropriate shoes. Remember to take a map of the trail, bug spray, flashlights, a first aid kit, and at least one canteen of water.

MUST HAVES
• *Map of the trail*
• *Bug spray*
• *Flashlights*
• *First aid kit (adhesive bandages, elastic bandages, bee sting kit, etc.)*
• *Water*

TO-DO LIST
• *Find and check out the trail.*
• *Arrange for a person who can identify plants and trees to join your group.*
• *Collect the necessary gear.*

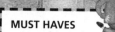

GO!

Before entering the trail, say: **Today we are getting two lessons in one day! But for now, I'm going to keep them a secret. Let's see if you can figure them out along the way.** (At this point, pull out a map which can be real or fake.) **OK, we've got a map! According to this map, we should come to a small footbridge in a short while. We don't have to get off the main path for any reason. There are no short-cuts. If our map is correct we will, in the end, do a loop and wind up right back where we started. If we hurry, we'll have time for a short game and a quick snack.**

As you hike, pace yourself so as not to finish too quickly. Allow the kids to enjoy God's wonderful nature. When you come to a connecting trail or fork in the road, pull out the map and begin to wonder aloud if taking a different trail may be faster or easier. Say: **Wow! We have been walking for some time. Maybe we should take this connecting trail. It is probably going where we want to go. And besides, it looks like an easier trail to walk. But then again, our map here shows the loop-trail. It shows that we are supposed to stay on this trail. Let's vote by a show of hands. How many of you think we should take this wider, easier trail? How many of you think we should stay on this trail which is clearly marked on the map? OK, we'll continue on this trail. I just hope that eventually we cross the bridge and reach our goal.**

When you reach the footbridge, say: **Finally! We have reached the bridge. It's a good thing we stayed on this path or we would have missed the bridge altogether. I know we were tempted to take the other trail, because it did look easier. But boy, am I glad we stuck it out! Hey, look under the bridge. I'm glad we**

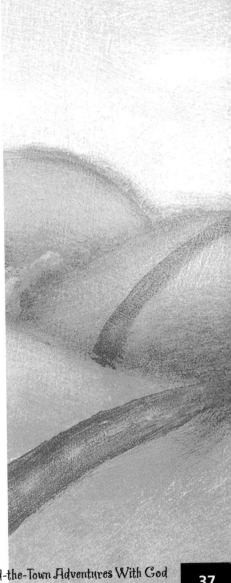

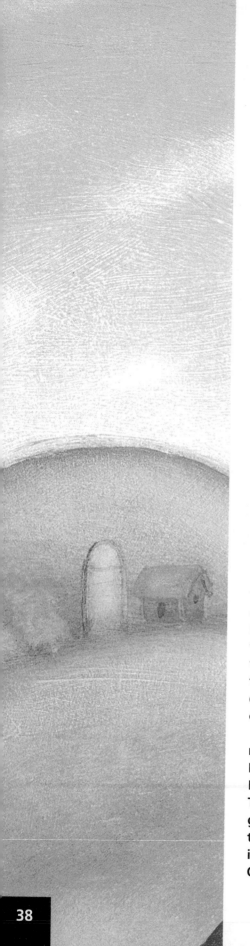

don't have to walk through that tough terrain. That would nearly make our journey impossible. Did you know God provided for us a bridge to Heaven? We'll talk about that later. But just remember that without a bridge we would be in big trouble.

When you have completed the loop, gather your kids for the rest of the lesson.

What Does God Say?

Say: Our journey was fun. We saw many different flowers, trees, and even insects. Did anyone else see other unique wildlife? (Allow children to share.) I'm glad we didn't choose to get off the path. We could have taken the other one, but who knows where that could have led us. Maybe to an area far from where we wanted to go!

Did you know that God's Word, the Bible, tells us that if we are truly seeking after him that it's like we are traveling on a narrow path? It may not be the easiest trail to take. In fact, it takes great discipline even to stay on this path. Temptations and forks in the road will try to distract you. The devil will use the evils of this world to try to get you to take his path. He may do this by luring you into loving money, sports, drugs, or anything more than God.

And when the devil gets you on his path, you will notice that many people take this journey. Why? Because it's an easy path. Look at what God says in Matthew 7:13, 14. "Enter through the narrow gate. The road that leads to hell is a very easy road. And the gate to hell is very wide. Many people enter through that gate. But the gate that opens the way to true life is very small. And the road to true life is very hard. Only a few people find that road" (ICB).

Trust me when I urge you to stay close to God and stay on the narrow path. The devil will do everything he can to get you on the other trail, but now you know the truth.

And what about the bridge? Without it, it would have been impossible for us to continue our journey. We needed that bridge to provide a way for us to travel safely over difficult or dangerous terrain. Without it, we might never have finished!

In the same way, did you know that Jesus is much like a bridge for us? He is the one who provides us access to God the Father and to Heaven. Without surrendering your life to him, there is no bridge, no passage to God. That's why Jesus said, "I am the way. And I am the truth and the life. The only way to the Father is through me" (John 14:6, ICB).

So if you want all that God has for you, do two things. First, stay on God's narrow path. Don't let anything sway you from living one hundred percent for God. Second, trust in Jesus as your bridge to Heaven. Nothing you can do in your own power will build a bridge to God. You must simply believe and trust in God's Son.

Wrap Up

To conclude this lesson, play the "Bridge Builders" game. The point of this game is to show how important Jesus' bridge is for our Christian walk. Close in a circle of prayer.

GAME—
BRIDGE BUILDERS
Have your group form a circle. Everyone must face the same direction as to be looking at the back of the head of the person standing in front of him. On your signal, everyone should sit on the lap of the person behind. If you build a successful bridge, no one should fall. Everyone must hold someone up or the bridge will collapse. The game is over when the bridge holds everyone!

AIRPORT

Focus: *Be strong and courageous.*
Scripture: *Joshua 1:9*

READY!

The airport is a unique setting to discuss fear. Flying in an airplane can be both exciting and scary. As your kids watch planes take off and land, you will find a great opportunity to talk about fear. This lesson will help you show your kids how to put their trust in God when they are afraid.

SET!

Schedule a tour at a local airport. Any airport, small or large, will do. Make arrangements to see three distinct areas: a hangar, the weather center, and the control tower.

GO!

Visit the three main parts of the airport and ask the following questions at the appropriate part.

Start with the hangar to show your kids where the planes are serviced and repaired. Help the group understand that in order for a plane to fly safely, it must be checked regularly and always kept in good condition.

1. Why is the hangar important? (It is the place to shelter, maintain, and repair airplanes.)

2. Where do Christians go to get shelter and be repaired? (God protects us if we trust him. He also gave us the church where we can get help from other Christians.)

3. What would happen if the planes were not checked and repaired regularly? (They would become unsafe to fly and could possibly malfunction or even crash.)

4. What would happen if Christians did not trust God or go to church regularly? (They might forget how much God loves them and how he will protect them when they are frightened. They might begin to do things that God wouldn't like or that would hurt them.)

Next, visit the weather center to show the kids the people and instruments that monitor the weather for the pilots. Help the group understand how important it is for a pilot to know the weather conditions at all times.

1. Why is the weather center important? (It helps pilots know what the weather is like where they are flying so that they can avoid storms and fly and land safely.)

2. How do Christians learn about dangers to avoid? (They go to church to learn from other Christians. They read the Bible to learn what God says to avoid.)

3. What might happen if pilots did not know what weather to expect? (They might fly into a bad storm or try to land at an airport that has bad weather making it dangerous to land.)

4. What would happen if Christians did not know about dangers in life? (They might make wrong decisions that would displease God or harm themselves or others.)

Finally, visit the control tower to show where the air traffic is directed.

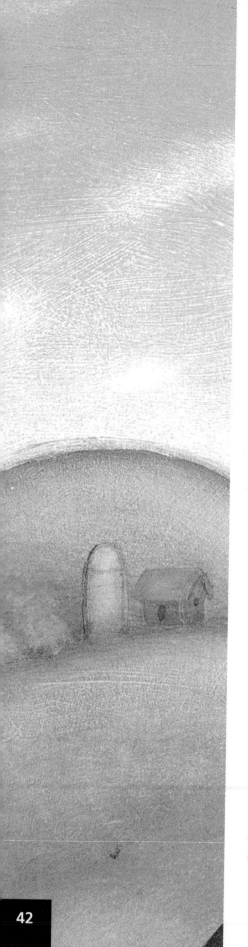

1. Why is the control tower important? (It helps pilots know where it is safe to fly. It gives pilots information about the airport so they know where and how to land.)

2. What would happen if there weren't an air traffic controller? (The pilots would not know what altitude is safe to fly, when it is safe to take off, or where it is safe to land.)

3. How do Christians get information about where it is safe to go and what is safe to do? (They go to church, read their Bible, and learn from other Christians.)

4. What is the controlling source of information? (God, Jesus, Holy Spirit)

After you have finished touring the airport, gather the kids into an empty concourse or waiting area and continue with the lesson. This is probably the best place to have your snack.

What Does God Say?

Summarize the events found in Joshua 1.

Say: **We can find a good example of someone who easily could have been afraid in a wonderful book in the Bible called Joshua. Joshua was Moses' assistant. When Moses died, Joshua was appointed to lead the people into the promised land. After they had roamed the desert for forty years, God told his people, the Hebrews, and their new leader, Joshua, that they should prepare to cross the Jordan River and enter into Canaan, which was the promised land. The Hebrews knew there would be battles to fight and wars to win, but could they do it? Here's what God said to Joshua at such a fearful moment in his life:**

"Remember that I commanded you to be strong and

brave. So don't be afraid. The Lord your God will be with you everywhere you go" (Joshua 1:9, ICB).

The Hebrews then crossed the Jordan River and claimed the promised land. God kept his promise. He aided and protected them every step of the way. Truly, they had no need to fear.

Often we are too afraid to let God have complete control of our fears. We try to work things out by ourselves and only get into worse trouble. God wants us to trust him when we are afraid or discouraged or in trouble. He wants to be our traffic controller.

Some of you may be living in fear. Maybe you are struggling in school, and you're afraid you may flunk. Others may be afraid because someone is bullying you. Maybe your parents are getting a divorce. The Bible proclaims that you do not need to be terrified. God will be with you in all circumstances!

Demonstrate the "Trust Fall" object lesson.

Wrap Up

Ask another brave volunteer to pray out loud that each person would trust God when they are afraid. Also thank God for the Bible and the church, which help us learn to trust God and show us dangers we should avoid.

OBJECT LESSON— TRUST FALL

Needed: *a blindfold, one child volunteer, and four adults chosen before the lesson without the child's knowledge.*

Set up: *Place the blindfold over the volunteer's eyes so he cannot see.*

Message: *In life, we need a hangar where we can go for service and repair; that is the church. The church and the Bible also serve as our weather center by warning us of the pitfalls and problems we might face. Then we need a traffic controller, Jesus. We have to trust him just as the pilots trust their air traffic controller.*

Prior to the lesson, arrange for the four adults to position themselves behind the volunteer on your signal. They should be instructed to catch the child when he falls back.

Say: **I have a very brave and trusting volunteer here. He has no idea what I am about to do. He does know, however, that we have been talking about fear! At this point he is beginning to feel a little anxious, and I believe his blood pressure is beginning to rise. Now, my very brave and trusting volunteer, in just a moment I will ask you to do something that will frighten you. You may be afraid, but remember: you are brave and trusting. God does not want you to live in fear or terror or discouragement. All I want you to do is trust me and then do what I ask you to do. It's as though you are giving your fear over to God. Instead of being afraid, you are trusting him!**

OK, are you ready to trust me? On the count of three, I want you to fall straight back.

Count to three. The child should fall back with the volunteers there to catch him. Remove the blindfold and ask the following questions:

What did you think when I asked you to fall back?

Were you afraid?

Did you find it hard to trust me?

Did you give your fear over to God?

CANDY STORE

MUST SEES
- Bulk candy
- Scales
- Display items
- Sales area

SNACK
A piece of candy, such as a sucker or jawbreaker, purchased at the candy store

Focus: *Don't give in to temptation.*
Scripture: *1 Corinthians 10:13*

READY!

There's just something about a candy store that makes anyone understand the concept of temptation. Just the thought of something that tastes as good as candy sometimes causes even adults to lose control. In a candy store, you can teach an effective lesson on identifying and resisting Satan's temptations.

SET!

Arrange for a tour of a candy shop. You should try to find one in a mall, because the object lesson requires visiting other stores in the mall. This trip should be one which encourages your children to use all five senses. Make sure your guide can show you where the candy is divided into smaller packages or stored prior to sale, and how it is weighed and sold. Arrange for the guide and all other employees in the store to offer candy to the children frequently; have them be as tempting as possible.

MUST HAVES
- 3x5 index cards
- Pencils
- A piece of hard candy for each child (purchased upon arriving at the store)

TO-DO LIST
- Arrange to have candy store staff tempt children with candy as they tour.
- Gather object lesson materials.

GO!

Upon arriving, tell the children they are allowed to look, smell, and listen, but they are not to touch or eat any candy—even if an employee of the store offers it or if it is just sitting there. Make a big deal about not taking or eating any candy, but do it only once at the very beginning, perhaps before you enter the store. Intensify the temptation by purchasing a piece of candy for each child. You would be wise in choosing a candy that will not make a mess, such as a jawbreaker or a sucker. Allow them to hold it, but remind them not to eat it until you tell them it is OK. As you tour the store, have the kids ask your guide various questions, for example:

1. **How many different candies do you sell?**
2. **What's the most expensive?**
3. **What's the most popular?**
4. **What's the most fattening?**
5. **Where are your various candies made?**

After your tour, do the object lesson on temptation. When the kids return, ask them why they think you have told them not to eat the piece of candy they have been holding for nearly half an hour. Also, ask if anyone was tempted to eat the candy. Did any of them lick the candy or put it into their mouth for only a second? Then continue the lesson.

What Does God Say?

Explain that just as they were tempted to eat the candy, so will they be tempted throughout life to do things which are against God's will and his plan for their life.

Read 1 Corinthians 10:13. Brainstorm some of the ways God provides a way out of falling into sin you are tempted to do.

Wrap Up

Close by allowing the children to eat their candy. As they are enjoying it, remind them how enjoyable sin can be, but like the candy, the enjoyment lasts only for a short time. Close in a circle of prayer.

OBJECT LESSON
Needed: 3x5 cards and pencils.
Set Up: none
Message: Resisting temptation is difficult, but the rewards are sweet.

Break up into groups of three to five with one or two adults supervising each group. Distribute 3x5 cards and pencils to each person. Give these instructions: **You have been divided into groups so that you may scavenge the shops in the mall. What you are looking for are things people are easily tempted to purchase or do instead of using their money wisely. You must write down your temptations in a list form. Each group must report back to the candy store in fifteen minutes. Compile your findings because only one list is needed for each group. Also, remember this: do not eat your candy yet.**

At the end of the fifteen-minute scavenger hunt, gather your children into a general meeting area in the candy store.

Have each group assign a speaker who can report what they found as "temptations" in the mall. Be sure they not only list the temptation, but also share why giving in to that temptation would be harmful if they chose that route.

GOLF RANGE

Focus: *Practice makes perfect.*
Scripture: *Philippians 3:14*

READY!

Hitting a golf ball correctly takes a lot of practice and patience. Pro golfers have committed their lives to working on their swing and accuracy of driving a ball toward the putting green. In fact, all pro golfers have spent thousands of hours perfecting their art. For those who have won professional tournaments, all would agree that practice makes perfect.

A lesson at the golf range will help your kids realize that the Christian walk takes practice. We can't hope to have growing relationships with Jesus if we don't take seriously our Bible study, prayer, and devotional life. Without practicing these "basics," a child of God will be frustrated much like a new golfer.

SET!

Arrange for a tour of a local driving range. Try to arrange it so that the kids will be allowed to walk the range to get a feel for the distance. Make sure they will be able to see the machines or devices used to collect golf balls from the range. Obtain the services of a well-above-average golfer. Many golf ranges have local professionals who frequent the facility. You may be able to enlist their help for the lesson.

GO!

After you have toured the range, gather your group behind one of the tee areas. Ask for a volunteer for the object lesson. When done, interview both your golfers, using the same questions for both. Have your guest golfer explain terms that the kids might not know.

1. **How many times have you golfed before?**
2. **What is your favorite course?**
3. **What is your best score?**
4. **Have you ever hit an eagle?**
5. **How many hours do you practice per week and how important is consistent practice to your game?**

Say: **To be a great golfer you must practice the basics. A golfer wears a glove to maintain a good grip on the club and to prevent blisters while swinging the club as many times as he does when playing or practicing. In fact, when he first starts practicing, blisters are often raised whether he wears the glove or not. But eventually, after learning the proper way to hold the club and to swing the club and after practicing many long hours, there are fewer blisters. At first it's quite painful, but soon it becomes more pleasant, as the difficulties become fewer—and that only comes after practice.**

When we first become Christians, it isn't always easy to do the things we know we ought to do. It's hard to break some of the bad habits we've developed; sometimes it seems quite painful to do the things we aren't used to doing. But after we've been going to church, praying, reading God's Word, or having devotions regularly it will become more natural and feel better—you'll find yourself wanting to do it more and more. Sure, you will never be truly perfect,

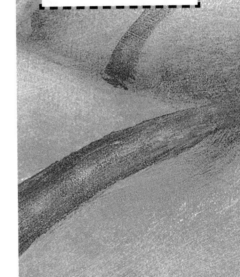

OBJECT LESSON

Ask for a volunteer who would like to attempt to hit a golf ball near the 50-yard marker. Be sure you choose a child with strong self-esteem or choose an adult who is not a good golfer.

Before allowing the volunteer to hit the ball, make sure he is "ready." Run him through some quick calisthenics, rub his shoulders and help him stretch out. Make a show of demonstrating the importance of being ready. Quickly spit-wash his golf ball and tee it up. Give the child binoculars and make sure he sees the target.

Demonstrate how to swing the club, stressing the importance of the follow-through.

When your volunteer attempts to hit the ball, chances are he will completely miss the ball or hit it nowhere near the marker. When children begin to laugh, be sure to channel the laughter toward "missing the ball" and not at the child directly. You may wish to ask other volunteers to attempt the same thing.

After the child has attempted to hit near the target, have your special guest golfer attempt to hit the mark. Have the guest show how to prepare to hit the ball properly. Hopefully, your guest golfer will be able to hit nearer the mark.

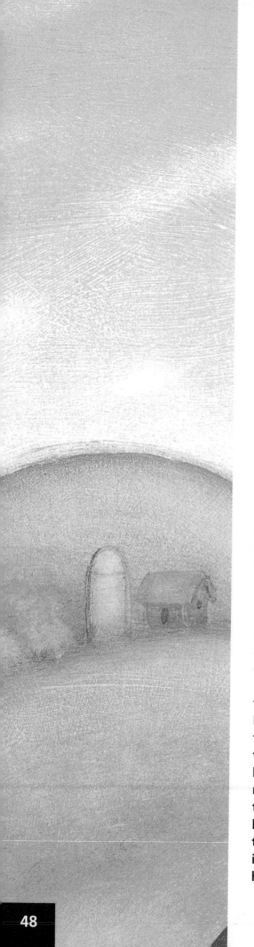

for everyone makes mistakes. But God wants you to take seriously the practice of growing closer to him each day you are alive.

A pro golfer spends endless hours learning the game. He does this because he wants to be the best, a champion! Today, I want to encourage you to become a champion for God. You won't even get close if your relationship to God only takes place on Sunday when you go to church. He expects you to draw near to him every day through prayer and devotion. In fact, God said in his Word, "Come near to God, and God will come near to you" (James 4:8, ICB).

Allow your children to try their skill at hitting a ball with the golf club. Be sure to have able adults ready to assist the children. Swinging a golf club wildly can be dangerous. You may wish to award a prize to the person who hits closest to the 50-yard marker.

What Does God Say?

Read Philippians 3:14: "I keep trying to reach the goal and get the prize. That prize is mine because God called me through Christ to the life above" (ICB).

Say: From reading this passage, one could agree that being a Christian is like a sport. There are the athletes, the referee, and a trophy or prize for those who finish in winning form. The big difference, however, is that the prize has already been won! Paul was telling his readers that the prize was already his. It's just a matter of receiving it at the end of the race. If we tried to run the race on our own, we would have no hope of winning it. Fortunately, Jesus has already run the race before us and won the prize for us; he's waiting at the end to give us the prize. Although the race has already been won by Jesus, it doesn't mean that

we can stop running or stop striving for the prize. We need to keep running, looking to Jesus for direction and as our inspiration, as our reason for running in the first place. The way we keep running, as if we are striving for the prize, is to keep practicing: reading our Bibles, praying, witnessing to our friends. If we continue to do these things, we're on the right track.

Wrap Up

Pass around a box of Wheaties cereal that has a picture of a renowned athlete on its front. Say: **All the athletes who are honored with their picture on the front of a box of Wheaties cereal have one thing in common: they are champions in their respective sport.**

Close in a circle of prayer asking God to help each person become a champion for Christ and take seriously the challenge that practice will make perfect.

SHOE STORE

MUST SEES
- Stock room
- Sales floor
- Brannock device (instrument to measure feet accurately)

SNACK
Red licorice strands (symbolic of shoelaces)

Focus: *Your faith must grow.*
Scripture: *Luke 2:40; 2 Peter 3:18*

READY!

Almost everyone wears shoes. They're what protect our fragile feet from injury or calluses. Shoes help us walk on rough ground or uneven terrain. Without shoes, we would always have to watch each step making sure not to walk on sharp pieces of glass, a bee, or some other object. But wearing the wrong size shoes can be worse than wearing no shoes at all. Indeed, as your feet grow in size, so must your shoes. A field trip to a local shoe store will be a great place to discuss with your group the importance of allowing your faith to grow as your years increase.

MUST HAVES
- Paper towels
- A pair of baby shoes
- A large shoe (the larger, the better)

TO-DO LIST
- Purchase paper towels.
- Collect items for object lesson (baby shoes, large shoe).
- Determine whether children can eat a snack within the store.

SET!

Arrange for a tour of a local shoe store. You should make sure the children will be able to see where the shoes are delivered, inventoried, and sold. Make sure the person who gives the tour is able to measure the children's feet with a Brannock device—some stores no longer use the device, but it is likely they will have one lying around. You'll want to be careful of giving the children their snack in the store, as sticky fingers may make the shoes unsalable. Be sure to get permission before allowing the children to eat in the store.

GO!

Before arriving at the store, give each child two paper towels. Have the children crumble each towel into a ball and stuff the wads into the toes of their shoes. You want to purposely make the shoes too small for the child's feet so as to add a small bit of discomfort. Have the children wear their shoes with the towels for a short while, at least for a little bit of walking.

Upon arriving at the shoe store, ask for a short tour of the stock room where trucks are unloaded and inventory is kept. Allow the children to ask your guide any questions they may have, or you may use these as starters:

1. **How many shoes are in your store?**
2. **Where are most shoes made?**
3. **What are the most popular shoes?**
4. **What are the most expensive shoes?**
5. **What is the largest shoe size you have sold?**
6. **How many pairs of shoes do you sell in a day, week, or year?**

Next, ask your guide to demonstrate how she measures a customer's feet for a new pair of shoes. You may wish for several of the children to have their feet measured.

Say: **Did you know that just as your feet have grown since last year, your faith is expected to grow also? God wants each of us to grow continually to be more like him. But some people, after asking Jesus to be their Savior, stop growing. They may neglect their devotional life and their prayer time, or they may get caught up in sin. Whatever the case, it is hard for God's Spirit to dwell in a person who does not wish to grow.**

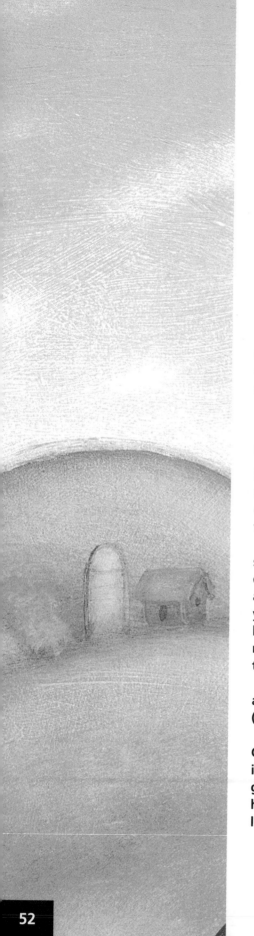

Before we came here, each of you stuffed your shoes with paper towels to make your shoes too tight. How did the tight squeeze feel? (Get a few responses.) Most of us would agree that we didn't like it. In the same way, it grieves God to live in a Christian who is not growing. In fact, it is unwise not to grow. Let me demonstrate why.

Do the "Baby Shoes" object lesson.

What Does God Say?

Say: Let's open our Bibles and see what God has to say about growth. First, let's read Luke 2:40: "The little child began to grow up. He became stronger and wiser, and God's blessings were with him" (ICB).

This verse refers to Jesus and tells us that he grew strong. This means he grew taller and bigger as each day passed. But it also means that Jesus grew spiritually, as well. He grew in favor with God, and at the young age of twelve was found to be in the Temple learning all he could about his heavenly Father. And notice that when Jesus was serious about growing, the grace or "favor" of God was upon him.

Next, let's look at 2 Peter 3:18: "Grow in the grace and knowledge of our Lord and Savior Jesus Christ" (ICB).

From this verse, it is important to understand that God expects you to grow in him. It is not an option; it is a command. He wants us to continually pray, study, go to church, love people, and devote ourselves to him. If we do these things, we will grow to be more like him.

Wrap Up

Pass around a very large shoe. Say: **Even though this shoe does not fit any of you now, it may some day after you have grown. In the same way, we all have areas in our spiritual life in which we can grow. Today, let's commit to ourselves, to each other, and to God that we will continue to grow in him.**

Close in a circle of prayer.

**OBJECT LESSON—
BABY SHOES**

Needed: A medium-sized child and a pair of very small baby shoes. Have the child sit in a chair as though being fitted for new shoes.

Set Up: Give the clerk a pair of baby shoes or have the clerk substitute baby shoes for the correct size.

Message: It's natural to grow, both physically and spiritually.

Say: *Let's pretend our volunteer is ready for a new pair of shoes. He's outgrown his old ones and is excited about putting on some new, comfortable, fashionable shoes. Now let's imagine that he has walked the aisles of this store, has made his choice, and has asked the sales person to retrieve his selection from the stockroom.*

The clerk will return with a box of shoes and should then elevate the volunteer's foot onto a stool. The clerk will then take the baby shoes out of the box and try to place the baby shoe on the volunteer's foot.

Obviously this shoe didn't fit. It was too small. Maybe at one time in this person's life this shoe would have fit, but not any more! Growth is natural; it's expected! It would be silly to think baby shoes would fit a person who is your age. In the same way, it would be wrong to stay at the same level of faith your whole life. Your faith should grow as you mature.

HELICOPTER LANDING PAD

Focus: *God answers prayers.*
Scripture: *1 Kings 18:17-38; James 5:16*

READY!

Taking your kids to a helicopter landing pad for a lesson on prayer may be the most exciting way to show them just how high the prayers of a righteous person ascend.

SET!

Most fairly large cities have a police helicopter unit or traffic control center. Many are willing to give public tours of their facilities. If you plan your meeting around the shift change, you may actually be able to see a helicopter land and another take off. With prior arrangements being made, some stations may offer a free ride on a helicopter to one of your children's leaders. This makes for a great opportunity to shoot some video or take pictures which can be shared later.

GO!

Take a tour of the heliport. Be sure to see the hangar where the helicopters are stored. If allowed, ask that a couple of children be strapped into a helicopter. Let them get the feel of what it might be like to be a pilot. After the tour, gather your group in an area to be seated. Involve your students in a discussion about prayer and the idea that God hears the prayers of the righteous.

Here are some discussion starters you may use:

1. Have you ever said a prayer and felt as though it went no higher than the ceiling? What do you think causes that?

2. Now consider the helicopter pilot and ground control. There is always constant contact between the two. Why is that? What does that teach us about prayer?

3. When a pilot is beginning to experience engine trouble, his first response is to call his superior officer who is on the ground. Why is that? How can this help him?

4. When we feel in trouble, what should be our first response?

What Does God Say?

Familiarize yourself with the story of Elijah on Mount Carmel found in 1 Kings 18:17-38. Retell the story to your group. Ask these questions:

1. Why were Elijah's prayers answered? (Because he was righteous; he believed in God's power.)

2. Why were the prayers of the prophets of Baal not answered? (Because their god was not real; they were unrighteous; they did not believe in the one, true God.)

3. What do we learn from this Bible story? (God answers the prayers of those who seek him with all their hearts.)

Do the object lesson.

Wrap Up

Gather in a circle. Have an adult volunteer pray that each child present would continue to grow in Christ and that each child will begin to realize the power of the prayers of a righteous kid.

OBJECT LESSON
Needed: Two volunteers, two balloons.
Set Up: One balloon is to be blown up by mouth and has "unrighteous" written on it with permanent marker. The other balloon is to be filled with helium and has "righteous" written across it using the same permanent marker. Have two children come forward. Each is to hold one balloon.
Message: The prayers of a righteous person are heard by God.
Say: In James 5:16 it says, "When a good man prays, great things happen" (ICB). In other words, the prayers spoken by a person who not only knows God but loves him are heard and answered. Have you ever wondered why some prayers never seem to be answered? Maybe it's because those who are saying the prayers are praying selfishly. Instead of praying for God's will, they pray for God to give them the things they really don't need! Other times, prayers are not answered because the person praying does not have a righteous relationship with Jesus! (Have the volunteer hold up the balloon which is labeled "unrighteous.")
Let's pretend this balloon represents the prayer of someone who does not know or follow God. It is the prayer of the unrighteous. (Have the person throw the balloon as high as possible.) *Notice that the prayers of the unrighteous fall to the ground and are not answered.* But let's see what happens to the prayers of the righteous, the person who is in tune with God. (Have the person simply release the balloon.) *See, the prayers of the righteous do ascend to Heaven.*

OPTOMETRIST'S OFFICE

Focus: *The blind need faith.*
Scripture: *Mark 10:46-52*

READY!

Your kids will enjoy a tour and lesson at the office of a local eye doctor. This is an ideal setting to study the life of blind Bartimaeus whose miraculous story is told in Mark's Gospel.

It might be difficult for some of us to relate to a blind man unless we were blindfolded. But consider the life Bartimaeus must have lived. He most likely needed help getting around and doing some of the basic, everyday things of life. He probably had to ask for help; in fact, he had to beg for money just to survive!

Still most of us can't relate. However, consider what the man said to Jesus in verse 51: "I want to see again!" (ICB). He had been able to see at one time, and now he was blind. Imagine the feelings of despair and hopelessness he must have felt not being able to do many of the things he could have done unaided. Now we begin to "see" as Bartimaeus did. We know the ways in which we have become "blinded."

Help your kids to understand what what kind of faith Bartimaeus must have had. He longed to be healed, to see again, and he just knew Jesus could help him. Help them understand that we know of ways that we need God's help and that all it takes is faith in Jesus to get that help.

SET!

Arrange for a tour of a local optometrist's office. Make sure at least some of the kids will be able to experience some of the tests done to check one's vision. You may be fortunate and find an eye doctor who would give a complete eye examination to one of your students. Be sure to get parental permission.

If frames and lenses are constructed at the location, a tour and demonstration of this would also be beneficial. Make sure you can see the waiting room, the examination room, the frame display room, and the lens grinding lab.

GO!

During and after the eye examination, allow the students to ask any questions they may have of the optometrist. After the tour, gather the kids into the showroom or another general meeting place. Continue the lesson by discussing the following questions:

1. What would it be like to be blind?
2. How would being blind effect what you do at home? At school?
3. Without sight, how would you distinguish between friends, family, etc.?
4. What other senses would become more important?

What Does God Say?

Share the story of blind Bartimaeus found in Mark 10:46-52. Say: **Being blind is difficult. Back in the days of Bartimaeus, blindness was seen as being a curse from God and not merely a medical condition. What**

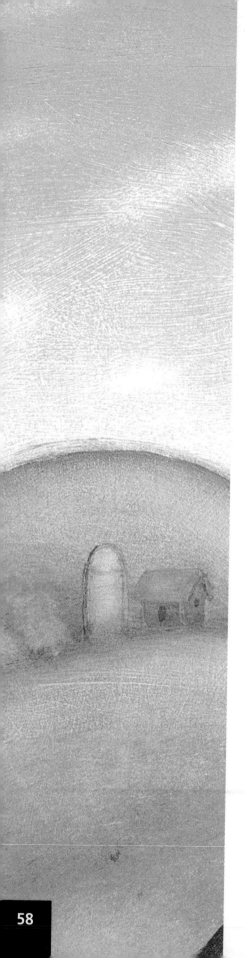

can we learn from blind Bartimaeus in Mark 10:46-52?

1. He was persistent. Bartimaeus was very insistent upon meeting Jesus. When the crowd told him to be quite, he wouldn't take "no" for an answer. In his mind, this was his one and only chance to bring his deepest, most desperate request to God. It was his persistence which helped a blind man see.

2. He was eager to meet Jesus. Bartimaeus didn't need to be told twice. When Jesus called him, he jumped to his feet and made a beeline to the Lord. He even left his coat which he threw off. Nothing was going to hold him back or slow him down when it came to meeting God. Sometimes we'll let things interfere with our getting to God. We'll play sports or watch TV instead of attending church.

3. He had a clear purpose. Bartimaeus knew that his sight was the one and only thing he wanted. He didn't ask for a new house, lots of wealth, or even daily necessities. He asked for his sight. When we come to God in prayer, if we are diligent and have God's will as our clear purpose, things will happen.

4. He had faith. Bartimaeus was healed, not because he was persistent, not because he jumped up when Jesus called him, and not because he knew what he wanted. Truly, he was healed because he had faith. Verse 52 says, "You are healed because you believed" (ICB).

Do the object lesson.

Wrap Up

Pass out the carrot sticks and allow the children to enjoy the crunchy snack. Say: **They say carrots are supposed to improve your vision. I doubt that a bushel would have helped poor Bartimaeus. He was blind** beyond repair. But look at what God could do for a simple man with lots of faith! Do you have faith? Do you believe God can help you? Oh, you may not be blind, but maybe you still need God's help. Perhaps you have a bad habit you can't seem to break. Or you may suffer from having a bad temper. Did you know that God can help? Take the example of Bartimaeus and apply it to your life. Be persistent. Know exactly what you want from him and, by all means, have lots of faith that God can help.

Go around the room and ask for prayer requests from children who need special help from God. When all requests have been listed, allow the children to pray aloud for each other's needs. Have one of the leaders conclude with a final prayer.

> **OBJECT LESSON**
> **Needed:** blindfolds
> **Set Up:** none
> **Message:** It is difficult to be blind and without help.
>
> Depending on the size of your group, blindfold some (or all) of your students. Make sure they cannot see. Use the exercise to show how difficult it is to be blind. Have your kids do the following:
>
> 1. Make a circle by holding hands.
> 2. Untie and tie their shoes.
> 3. Find someone who is wearing red clothing.
> 4. Ask kids to describe the carpet or wallpaper in the office area.
> 5. Have kids line up shortest to tallest in size.
> 6. Find and grab a neighbor's ear.

FIRE STATION

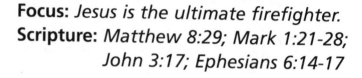

MUST SEES
- Sleeping quarters
- Kitchen
- Garage
- Trucks
- Equipment
- Firefighter's clothing and gear

SNACK
Fireball candy or cinnamon gum

MUST HAVES
- Various trivets and hot-dish mats

TO-DO LIST
- Arrange for a demonstration of putting out a fire.
- Gather the materials for the object lesson.

Focus: *Jesus is the ultimate firefighter.*
Scripture: *Matthew 8:29; Mark 1:21-28; John 3:17; Ephesians 6:14-17*

READY!

Kids love firefighters. The fact that they are trained protectors of all that is vulnerable to flames makes them special in the eyes of children. And so it is true that without firefighters our world would be a much more unsafe place. Who would stop forest fires when lightning strikes? Who would extinguish the flames that engulf a house because of a bad electrical connection? Unless these trained professionals are in place and ready, we would be in trouble. Truly, they stand between us and utter destruction.

In the same way, Jesus is our protector. He stands between us and the fiery darts of the devil. He is the ultimate firefighter. A trip to a local fire station will allow your children to understand just how important Jesus' role is in our lives. Without him, we are in grave danger.

SET!

Arrange for a tour of a local fire station. Make sure that the kids will be able to see the equipment, the firefighter's clothing and gear, the sleeping quarters, the kitchen, the garage, and any kind of training facilities. Try to arrange for the children to be able to try on some of the gear or at least see how some of it works. Perhaps the guide can arrange for a demonstration of how the firefighters put out a fire.

GO!

Tour the entire fire station. Be sure the fire chief or another firefighter shows you the living quarters, the workout room, the offices, and finally end up where the fire engines and all the gear are kept. Arrange for a firefighter to give a short talk on what to do if you catch on fire. He may even have some of the children do the exercise "stop, drop, and roll." Also, be sure to ask that some or all of the children be allowed to try on some of the gear, such as coat, pants, and helmet. They also may be permitted to board the fire engine. As you tour the station, ask these questions or any other questions the children may have:

1. **What causes most house fires?**

2. **What is the best thing we can do if there is a fire at our home?**

3. **Why is it smart not to play with matches?**

4. **How many fires does this station put out in a week or year?**

5. **Have you ever been burned while putting out a fire?**

6. **What's a fireman's best protection against the flames?**

After the tour is complete, gather your group into a general meeting area where they can sit and participate in the object lesson.

What Does God Say?

Say: **Did you know that the Bible says we have a protector who stands between us and the devil? With Jesus on our side, we are sure to defeat the destruction Satan wants to bring our way. James 4:7 says, "Give yourselves to God. Stand against the devil, and the**

OBJECT LESSON
Needed: *various trivets or hot-dish mats*
Set Up: *none*
Message: *Sometimes it is necessary to put something between you and potential danger in order to protect yourself.*

Say: ***There are many different kinds of trivets or hot-dish mats in this world. Some are made of wicker, while others are made of ceramic tile. Still others are made of thick cloth. Do you know what these are for? Are they simply for decoration? Of course not. They are used to protect your tables and counters when you need to set down a hot pan, dish, or skillet. Sometimes the dish is hot enough to damage the table's finish or scorch the table itself. The trivets and mats stand between the finish of the table and the hot dish. The trivets and mats serve the same purpose as the firefighter's coat. Just as the mats protect the table, the fire coat protects the firefighter from the intense heat and flames.***

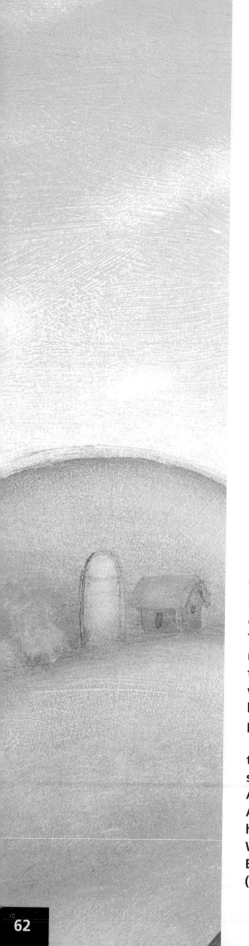

devil will run away from you" (ICB). There's nothing more the devil would like than to see you spend eternity with him in Hell. But God has a different plan for you. He wants you to be free from Satan's bondage.

Matthew tells the true story of two men who were controlled by Satan's evil spirits. When the evil spirits took one look at Jesus, they shouted, "What do you want with us, Son of God?" (Matthew 8:29, ICB).

Obviously these evil spirits did not want to mess with Jesus. They knew of his power. At the same time, they wanted to rule the lives of the two men they possessed. So what did Jesus do? He cast the evil spirits into a herd of pigs who then plunged themselves into a lake and were drowned.

Another time is recorded in Mark 1:21-28. In the local synagogue, Jesus met a man who was controlled by the devil. The devil cried out, "Jesus of Nazareth! What do you want with us? Did you come to destroy us? I know who you are—God's Holy One!" (ICB). The devil wanted to be left alone to torment the man. That's when Jesus simply said to the evil spirit to say no more and to come out of the man. The spirit shook the man and came out of him with a shriek. The devil would like to do what he wishes to do with your life, but Jesus will stand between you and Satan. He will protect you.

In fact, God has given us protection very similar to that of a fireman. Ephesians 6:14-17 says: "So stand strong, with the belt of truth tied around your waist. And on your chest wear the protection of right living. And on your feet wear the Good News of peace to help you stand strong. And also use the shield of faith. With that you can stop all the burning arrows of the Evil One. Accept God's salvation to be your helmet" (ICB).

Each of these pieces of God's armor is similar to the equipment of a firefighter, and each is something that we get through Jesus, who stands between us and the devil. The truth—like a belt—holds all of Jesus' teachings together in our lives. And with that truth, we know how to live right—just as Jesus has commanded us—which protects us from the devil's temptations. The Good News of Jesus' death and resurrection to save us helps us stomp out the little fires that sometimes keep us from walking with Jesus. Our faith in Jesus to save us helps us to avoid the temptations the devil throws at us like burning arrows. And the salvation we receive through Jesus gives us eternal life, just as the fireman's helmet helps give him protection and life-giving oxygen.

Wrap Up

Say: **So why do so many kids not trust and believe in God? Maybe it's because they think it's fun and exciting to live close to the edge of danger. I encourage you to put your trust and faith in God. Be sure to let him protect you. Remember, the Bible says in John 3:17, "God did not send his Son into the world to judge the world guilty, but to save the world through him" (ICB).**

Close in a circle of prayer.

DENTIST'S OFFICE

Focus: *Prevent "truth decay."*
Scripture: *Matthew 6:19, 20*

READY!

Every so often, we all have to go to the dentist's office. As much as we may not like it, it is a reality of life. If we have taken care of our teeth by brushing, flossing, and eating few sweets, our teeth will most likely be decay-free. But for those who do not brush between meals, floss each day, or watch the amount of candy, cake, and pop they consume, they may very well have cavities.

A lesson at the local dentist's office can be a great object lesson as to how important it is to continually take care of our spiritual life. Just as the person who doesn't take proper care of her teeth is subject to tooth decay, the person who is undevotional, skips church regularly, and doesn't cultivate her relationship with Christ is subject to spiritual decay.

The devil doesn't have to knock out our spiritual "teeth" to get the best of us. All he has to do is convince us that it's not important to seek God's will for our lives daily or to pray continually. The little things, a weak spot here or a tiny crack there, just as with our teeth, let in just enough sin to start the terrible process of "truth decay."

Help your kids realize that while some of these things seem innocent at first, they start to compound the problems and make other small cracks get bigger. Also help them to realize that Jesus not only prevents further decay, he can fix the "cavities" that have already formed.

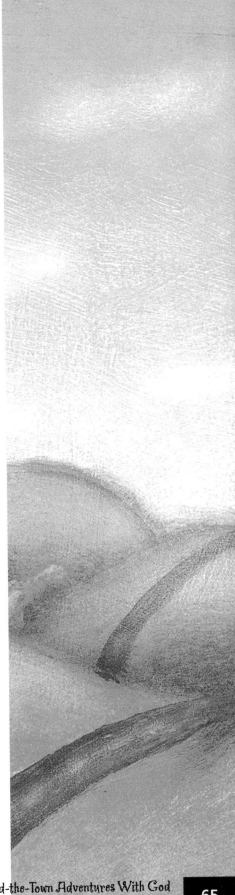

SET!

Ask for a tour of the dentist's office. Request to see the various kinds of equipment the dentist uses on her patients. Ask specifically to see the X-ray room, the waiting room, the records room, and the examination room.

Make sure the dentist giving the tour will demonstrate how to brush properly and help you and your kids better understand what causes decay. With proper authorization, the dentist may even be willing to give a demonstration of how she cleans teeth. One of your students may already be her patient, and the dentist may be willing to show some simple cleaning on the child's teeth. It is important to be sure that the dentist, patient, and parents are comfortable with such an arrangement. Be sure to have written permission from parents.

GO!

Visit the dentist's office. After the tour, gather the children into the waiting room for the rest of the lesson. Begin by reviewing what the dentist said was important in taking care of your teeth. Ask these questions:

1. **Why is it important to take care of your teeth?**

2. **If you have a serious cavity and you have the tooth pulled, will it grow back?**

3. **Why is the calcium found in milk and the fluoride found in toothpaste so important?**

4. **How do they both protect your teeth?**

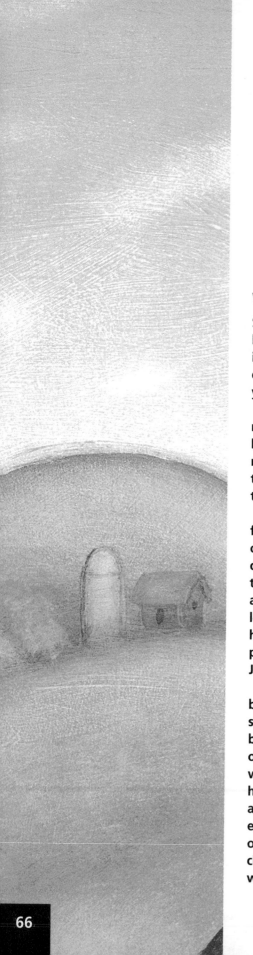

What Does God Say?

Say: What does God have to say about decay? Let's look at Matthew 6:19, 20. Here Jesus recognizes the importance of taking care of things which will last for eternity. Your soul is the most important possession you have. You would be wise to take care of it!

You see, everything else will eventually decay. Cars rust; toys break; buildings crumble. But your soul will last forever. So why do so many children and adults neglect their spiritual life? Why do they let their relationship with Jesus decay? Well, that's a good question!

For those kids who always eat sweets and junk food, they hardly ever think about the consequences of their poor eating habits. It's not until they get a check-up or have a toothache that they realize their teeth are in trouble. In the same way, many people allow sin and disobedience to eat away slowly at their love and devotion to Jesus. They start skipping church, hanging out with the wrong crowd, and neglecting to pray. Before you know it, they are no longer following Jesus.

There are also some signs that something is wrong, but you have to be looking for them. Just as you should see some signs of problems with your teeth: bleeding or sore gums, bad breath, pain when you eat or drink; you should be able to notice things going wrong with your spiritual life: finding it easier to sin, having problems with your relationships with friends and family members. God also gives us help from others. Just as a friend might offer a piece of gum to help our bad breath, he might also offer to pick you up for church if you start missing frequently or ask to pray with you about a problem you might be having.

Be sure to invest in things that will last for all eternity. Don't let your spiritual life decay!

Do the object lesson.

Wrap Up

Give each child a 10-inch piece of dental floss to tie into a bracelet. As you close in prayer, tell the children that every time they see the bracelet on their wrist, they should remember to always do their best to prevent spiritual decay.

OBJECT LESSON

Needed: two bananas, one that is ripe and ready to eat and another that is rotten and "yucky"

Set Up: none

Message: If you want to have a healthy relationship with God, you will have to work at keeping it healthy.

Hold up the first banana and say: **Look at this ripe banana. It is perfect in every way. When I peel this banana, notice how there are no dark spots on it. It has been cared for properly.**

Then, hold up the second banana and say: **Look at this banana. It has been dropped, smashed, and abused. When I open it, notice the brown, rotten spots. This banana is overly ripe and not much good for anything.**

Some of you have taken good care of your relationship with Jesus. You have spent time reading his Word, the Bible. You pray and go to church to worship and learn. That's how you prevent spiritual decay. But others of you have become lax about being alone with God so that now you can't hear His voice. Oh, you may go to church and even pray before your meals, but for some, those things are done out of habit, not out of love and adoration.

Today, you have seen the effects of tooth decay. You can prevent it. You have also seen the effects of spiritual decay. You can prevent it! Will you?

POTTERY SHOP

MUST SEES
- Clay storage
- Pottery wheel
- Kiln
- Painting and glazing area

SNACK
Fudge (because of its clay-like consistency) or gingerbread people (to represent shaped and molded people)

Focus: *You are shaped and molded in God's hands.*

Scripture: *Jeremiah 18:3-6; Isaiah 64:6, 8*

READY!

In God's Word, the Bible, we learn that his children are much like a hunk of clay in the potter's hands. He continually shapes and molds us into his image. Yes, at times this process can be hard, but the potter sees what this clay can become with a little bit of work. And because of that the potter never gives up. He works the clay until it becomes beautiful and useful to the Kingdom.

A trip to the local pottery shop will allow for a great lesson on how God continues to shape and mold us until we resemble him. With some planning, your group may even get to create their own pieces of pottery.

MUST HAVES
- Clay
- Finished pottery
- Broken pottery

TO-DO LIST
- Determine whether children will be able to make and fire a piece of pottery.
- Arrange for the demonstration for the object lesson.

SET!

Set up a tour at a pottery shop. Make sure the children will see the area where pottery is made, fired, painted and glazed, and sold. You may need to search for a local artist who works in clay or find a school where pottery is taught. If at all possible, arrange for each child to shape and form a piece of pottery which would be fired and available for pickup at a later time.

Prior to your field trip, set up a demonstration with someone at the pottery shop. Design the experience so that you can add commentary at each point of the demonstration. The idea will be to take a piece of unformed clay and mold it into a beautiful, useful vessel. The added commentary will share the parallel of how God shapes and molds us to completion.

GO!

Tour the pottery shop. Make sure the children see the entire process of creating beautiful pottery. They should see the clay in its original form, as it is being kneaded, as it is thrown, as it is painted or glazed, and as it is fired. Perhaps they can see a class in session or see a number of potters at work. As they watch the object lesson demonstrated, try to give a running commentary as is outlined in the next section.

What Does God Say?

Hold up a lump of clay. Say: **Look at this lump of clay. In its current condition it is basically useless. But with a little work and vision, a potter can take a lump of clay and make it into something amazing. God's Word teaches that you and I are a lot like clay. Without the potter's help, we are useless. Isaiah 64:6, 8 says, "All of us are dirty with sin. All the right things we have done are like filthy pieces of cloth. . . . But Lord, you are our father. We are like clay, and you are the potter. Your hands made us all" (ICB).**

One of the first things the potter does with clay is knead it as a baker does with dough. By doing this, the potter removes air pockets and any lumps which could destroy the pot before it is even finished. If we are like clay and God is the potter, it makes sense that he would help remove our impurities. First John states that if we are in the light and have been cleansed by Jesus' blood, then he purifies us from all sin.

When the clay is put on the potter's wheel, it is centered. That means the potter makes sure the clay is exactly in the middle. If it is not positioned precisely, the clay will wobble when the wheel is put into

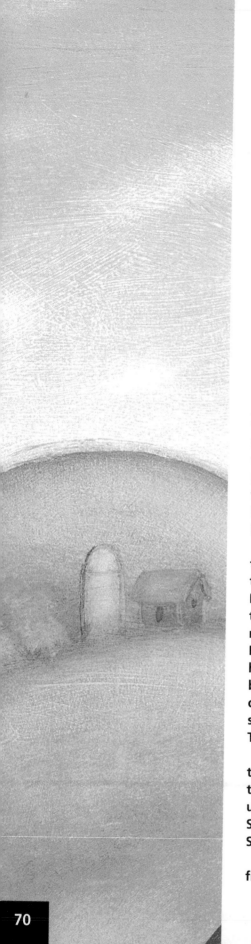

motion. It will be difficult to shape. In the same way, if we are not in the center of God's will for our lives, we will collapse and fall apart when problems come our way. If we are centered, we will have stability to hold on during life's toughest trials.

Once the wheel begins to spin, the potter uses his hands to shape the pot. Slowly the pot will take on a more definite shape. It's the potter's creativity and vision which determines the shape of the pot. Romans 9:21 asks an interesting question: "Does not the potter have the right to make out of the same lump of clay some pottery for noble purposes and some for common use?" (NIV). Wouldn't it be strange for the clay to jump off the wheel and argue with the potter? — "Hey you can't do that? Ooh that hurt! Stop that!" It is no less strange for us to question God about our lives than it is for a pot to jump off the wheel and ask the potter what it is he thinks he is doing. We should trust the process God is putting us through. It is molding us into the image of Jesus. God knows what he is doing. He won't cause us to become something unusable.

After the walls of the pot have been raised, the potter begins the trimming process. He removes any excess, the parts which are unnecessary. The pot is now formed. It has taken on shape, and it's ready for the finishing touches. A careful hand is needed here. The slightest mistake can leave permanent scars on the vessel. Why? Because even though the pot is shaped, it is neither hard nor mature. In the same way, kids, you need to be very careful not to get caught up in the wrong crowd while in your youth. You can easily find yourself stumbling into sinful situations before you know it! Truly, you can be scarred for life if you are not careful.

The next step is called the sealing process in which the vessel is coated and becomes able to hold water. If this process were skipped, the finished pot would be unable to do its job. In the Christian life, the Holy Spirit is our sealer. He seals our salvation. By the Holy Spirit we know that Jesus lives in our lives.

After the pot has been sealed, it is then ready to be fired. Forming the pot may only take fifteen or twenty minutes, but firing the pot may take fifteen to twenty hours. Shadrach, Meschach, and Abednego were placed in fire, and they stood strong for their faith. At some point all Christians will be tested. If you can hold firm for God, you will be a useful tool for his cause.

Unfortunately, some pots never make it to the stage of usefulness. Instead, ruined pots are thrown back into the potter's field. The potter's field is a piece of ground that isn't suitable for building or agricultural purposes, because of the high clay content of its soil. Broken and useless pieces are heaped into (more or less) a junk pile. All around us there are human junk piles, lives that have been so ruined by sin that they are no longer good to themselves or anyone else.

With the pot, it's pretty much hopeless. Once it's been tossed into the potter's heap, that is the end of it, until it has been broken down completely and becomes part of the soil again. It will not be of use to the potter until it has been completely broken down.

In the same way, God can restore and rescue any human life. Anyone who will come to him and turn away from sin can find a new beginning. Just as the pottery has to be broken down completely, sin will leave its scars, but remember, God can make any sin-scarred life soft and pliable in his hands and use it again.

So, what about you? Are you useful to God? Can he trust you to stand tall and proud for him? Or is your spiritual life in the trash pile, no good to yourself or anyone else? I'll let you answer those questions yourself, silently.

Wrap Up

Say: Tonight I want to invite those of you who don't know Christ to come to him. I want to invite those of you who have turned away from him to come back. I want to encourage you who are going through the molding and purifying process to stay pliable and soft in his hand. And, finally, for those of you who are in the fire, I invite you to recognize God's presence there and rejoice.

*Special thanks is given to Train Depot for permission to use their lesson "The Potter's Process" from their Life Curriculum.

AIRPLANE PREFLIGHT CHECK

Focus: *Know and follow the Ten Commandments*
Scripture: *Exodus 20:1-17*

READY!

Prior to takeoff, the airplane's mechanical condition must be perfect. That is why a preflight check is vital. A long list of safety points must be studied by experienced airplane mechanics and pilots to make sure that all of the parts of the airplane are working properly. The fluids and air pressure are topped off, and then the plane is approved for flight. We might call this checklist a set of commandments.

It's good to have a guide, list, or set of laws to serve as a checklist. God has given us a list of things to consider as we walk with him daily. They are called the Ten Commandments! They were first given to the people of Israel so they would have a guide to help them navigate their way through the trials and struggles of this world.

This lesson can be used to help your children realize the importance of not only knowing the Ten Commandments, but also the importance of practicing them in their daily lives. The Ten Commandments are our own preflight checklist.

SET!

Arrange a lesson with a local pilot who owns or has access to a small two- or four-seat airplane. Ask him to give your group a demonstration of what takes place during a preflight inspection. Perhaps he can show the children his checklist of all the fluids and working parts of the plane (his list of commandments). Also, it may be possible for some of the children to check various parts after the pilot has done the complete check.

If possible and if time permits, arrange for the pilot to take one or two children for a short ride, at least across the field and back. You could draw names out of a hat to determine which children get to go. Be sure to have written parental permission before allowing any children to board the plane.

GO!

Have a local pilot demonstrate the procedures for checking an airplane prior to flight. If it is possible, have him give a few children a brief ride in the plane. When the plane returns, be sure to interview the pilot and the children who went. You may wish to ask these questions of the pilot.

1. **How long does it take to become a pilot?**
2. **How fast does your plane go?**
3. **Why is the preflight check so important?**
4. **How far can you see from your plane on a clear day?**

You may want to ask these questions of the children who took the airplane ride:

1. **Have you ever been on an airplane before?**
2. **Did you feel safe? Why or why not?**

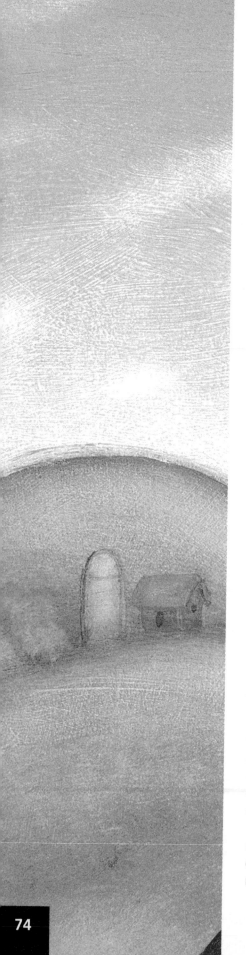

3. Would you like to become a pilot?

After this has been done, gather the children in a general meeting area. A lobby or a hangar would do nicely.

What Does God Say?

Say: **Today we have been talking about the importance of the preflight check. Without doing a preflight check, the pilot endangers not only himself and his passengers, but also people on the ground. All of us have seen TV news reports of planes that have crashed because of "pilot error." Many of these crashes could have been avoided if the pilot would have been thorough in his preflight examination.**

The Bible, God's Word, says that the Lord gave the Israelites a list of rules or laws to serve as a "preflight check." It is a brief checklist to keep them from "crashing" due to error. It is found in Exodus 20:1-17. The Ten Commandments were given to Moses, the leader of the Israelites, while they were on the brink of making their flight into the promised land: Canaan.

God knew that many things could go wrong for his children if they did not stay close to him. This decree from God, the Ten Commandments, was so vital that he told the Israelites: "Be careful. Do what the Lord your God has commanded you. You must follow the commands exactly. Live the way the Lord your God has commanded you. Then you will live and be successful. You will live a long time in the land you will own" Deuteronomy 5:32, 33 (ICB).

Notice that God didn't tell the Israelites simply to memorize the Laws; he told them to obey the Laws exactly. Sometimes we think of the Ten Commandments as the Ten Suggestions, thinking that we can get

by with doing only halfway the things God wants us to do. The Israelites soon found out the hard way that breaking God's commands or even bending them just a little bit is enough to cause terrible consequences, the most serious of which is being a sinner before God.

The Israelites often neglected obeying the Law because they thought it was enough simply to know or possess the Laws. Christians sometimes do the same thing. Sometimes we think it is enough to possess God's Word or to read the Bible every day or to go to church every Sunday. But that's not what saves us. It is true that when we accept God's gracious salvation through faith in Jesus, we are no longer judged by how we keep God's commands, although often there are still consequences to breaking these commands. However, we must still strive to do the things God wants us to do, if not simply to obey God, at least to show that we are thankful for his grace and that we love him. When we constantly seek to obey God's commands, we are less likely to break them and suffer the consequences that occur.

Have the children take the "Ten Commandments Quiz."

Wrap Up

Say: **Today we learned that if a pilot forgets to check even one thing on his plane, it can cause disaster. Also, if we do not know and then follow God's Word, especially the Ten Commandments, that, too, can cause disaster. This week, open your Bible to Exodus 20 and Deuteronomy 5 and learn God's preflight checklist!** Close in a circle of prayer.

**ACTIVITY—
TEN COMMANDMENTS
QUIZ**

Hand out the pencils and a 4x6 card to each child.

Say: I would never want to embarrass you in front of your peers. However, we are going to take a private test. I want you to list as many of the Ten Commandments as you can remember, even if it's just one or two. Be sure not to look at your friend's card. Don't worry; we will not read your card aloud.

Give your children a few minutes to complete the exercise. Then begin to list the commandments as the children speak them out until you get all ten. Have a Bible or a backup list ready so you don't miss any. Ask for a show of hands of how many children missed at least one of the Ten Commandments.

**TEN COMMANDMENTS
"CHECKLIST"**

Exodus 20:3-17 (ICB)

1. "You must not have any other gods except me."

2. "You must not make for yourselves any idols."

3. "You must not use the name of the Lord your God thoughtlessly."

4. "Remember to keep the Sabbath as a holy day."

5. "Honor your father and your mother."

6. "You must not murder anyone."

7. "You must not be guilty of adultery."

8. "You must not steal."

9. "You must not tell lies about your neighbor in court."

10. "You must not want to take anything that belongs to your neighbor."

FISHING HOLE

MUST SEES
- *Different types of fishing rods and reels*
- *Nets*
- *Tackle box*
- *Bait*
- *Lures*

SNACK
Goldfish crackers

Focus: *You are to be fishers of men.*
Scripture: *Mark 1:17*

READY!

Jesus has called each of us to be fishers of men. By that statement, he meant that we should take seriously helping those in need and sharing the love of Jesus with those with whom we come in contact so they will come to know him. And with Jesus' example in the Bible, we can learn to do just that.

A nearby fishing hole, stream, or lake is the perfect setting, not only to do a little fishing, but also to explain this key spiritual truth. Indeed, we were put on this earth for more than mere existence. God expects us to win the lost and pull in our nets as we fish for the sinners of this world.

MUST HAVES
- *Necessary fishing equipment*
- *First aid kit*
- *3x5 cards and pencils*

TO-DO LIST
- *Arrange for the proper licenses for you and other adults.*
- *Announce well in advance of the trip that the kids will be able to bring their own fishing pole for the trip.*
- *Arrange for transportation for all the equipment.*

SET!

Arrange to take your group to a local fishing hole, stream or lake. Make sure that all the kids are reminded to bring their fishing pole for the trip; in order to reduce the need for additional transportation, you may want to ask that children not bring any additional tackle boxes, lures, nets, etc. Also, to reduce the amount of additional equipment and mess, you may want to supply the bait, tackle box, rubber gloves, and a first-aid kit in case someone is injured.

You'll need to check your local laws about fishing to see who needs licenses. Most states allow children up to a certain age to fish without a license. Some states require that any adults accompanying children must be licensed.

GO!

When you get to the fishing location, say: **Today, our lesson is simply on fishing. For the next twenty minutes, I want you to simply do that—fish! Be sure to fish safely, watching how you cast your line. Two keys to fishing are this:**

    1. Use the right kind of bait.

    2. Be patient.

After twenty minutes of fishing, gather the kids into a general meeting area for the lesson. Be sure to brag on those who actually did catch a fish and begin the lesson by interviewing some of the kids. Here are some questions you can use:

    1. Why do you like fishing?

    2. Is it always exciting?

    3. Why is it important to use the right bait?

    4. What happens when you don't use the right bait?

    5. How does it feel to actually pull in and catch a fish?

For the last two questions, hand out 3x5 cards and pencils. When everyone has a card and pencil, ask these questions and have the children write down their answers.

    1. Why did Jesus tell his disciples to be fishers of men?

    2. How are you a fisher of men?

When the cards have been filled out and turned in, share some of the responses.

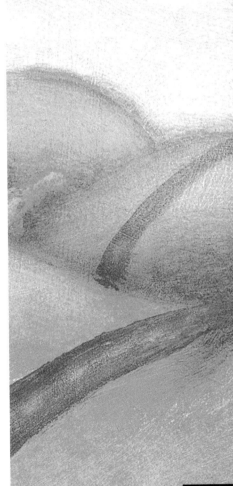

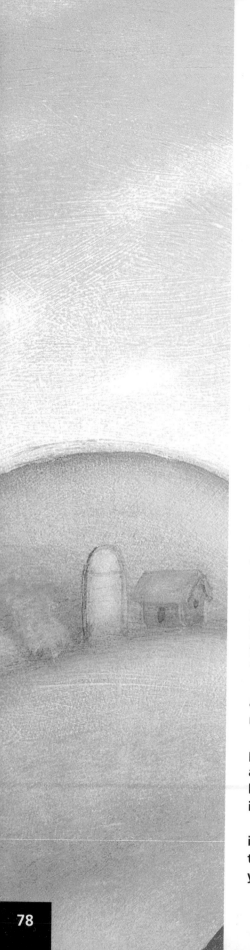

What Does God Say?

Say: What many good Christians miss in their spiritual walk is realizing that they were placed here on this earth for a purpose. Many Christians simply exist—living day-to-day—never concerned about anyone but their family and friends. But the Bible commands us to seek out the lost and share Jesus Christ with them. You see, life is more than just living day-to-day. It's sharing with others that Jesus died to save all people from their sins.

If you have ever been lost in the store, mall, or park, you know what a relief it is when you are found. Can you imagine the relief for someone who was lost in sin only to have a friend share with them the love of Jesus? Truly that friend has helped to save them from Hell.

In school, it's easy to hang around with only your friends, people you feel comfortable being around. But in Mark 1:17, Jesus told his disciples they would have to break free from their comfort zone and fish for the lost sinners. They were to become the first "fishers of men."

When you take seriously God's call to win the lost and become fishers of men, there are two things you need to know:

1. You must use the right bait. By this, I mean that people are only going to know Jesus if they see him alive in you. That will attract them. Be sure your life is being lived to its fullest. Make sure your light is shining brightly.

2. Be patient! All fishermen know that you don't pull in fish after only a minute or two of fishing. It takes time to catch fish. In the same way, it takes time to win your friends, but don't become discouraged when

doing God's work. If you are using the right bait and you are being patient, you will eventually see results.

Wrap Up

Close in a circle of prayer. Pray to God for the power to witness and the salvation of lost friends, family, and strangers.

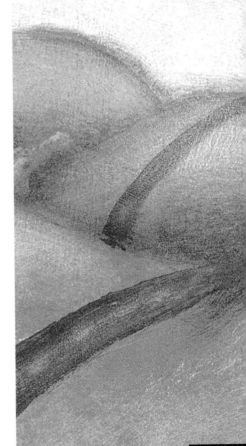

LIBRARY

Focus: *Read and know God's Word.*
Scripture: *Romans 15:4*

READY!

There are thirty-nine books in the Old Testament and
twenty-seven books in the New Testament. Together,
they total sixty-six books which make up the Bible. The
Bible, which was given to man by God's holy inspiration has a central message of salvation. It is that message which has changed the hearts and lives of complete civilizations as well as brought about the church
as we know it today. Many historians agree that it is
the most important book ever to have been written.
With that being stated, it should also be known that
this best-selling document is perhaps the least read
book or least understood book in history.

   With the public or private library as your surround-
ing, it is an ideal place for a lesson on the importance
of reading God's Word.

SET!

Begin with a tour of a large public library. Ask to see
how the books are checked in and out. Ask for a simple explanation of how the Dewey decimal system
works. Finally, ask to see the most valuable of all the
library's books. Most likely they will be in the
archives.

GO!

After you have completed your tour of the library, gather your kids in a general meeting area for the lesson. Begin by asking the children and adults what they would consider being the most important books or documents ever to be written. Here is a sample list:

- The Ten Commandments
- The Bible
- The Declaration of Independence
- The U.S. Constitution
- *Uncle Tom's Cabin*

Do the "Flaming Bible" object lesson. After the object lesson, hold up a Bible and say: **In Psalm 119:89, the Bible tells us, "Lord, your word is everlasting. It continues forever in heaven" (ICB). This book—and the words in it—is the only book which will last forever. It's an important book with an important message. Romans 15:4 tells us that "Everything that was written in the past was written to teach us, so that we could have hope. That hope comes from the patience and encouragement that the Scriptures gives us." The Bible's everlasting message is meant to give us hope and to encourage us.**

Have your children do the "Making a Book" activity. After the activity, say: **The Bible has as simple a message as some of your books as already stated. It is a message of God's love for those lost in sin and defeated by the devil. It would do you well to study the Bible so you can begin to understand and know the author, God himself.**

Wrap Up

Have the children sit in a circle. Open your Bible to John 3:16 and pass it around. Have each child read one word in the sentence until the complete verse has been read. Say: **This verse, in a nutshell, is the very message of the Bible. Let's commit ourselves not only to reading the Bible and getting to know the author better, but also to sharing this important message with others.**

Close in a circle of prayer. Pray for each child by name that God would reveal himself to them through the reading of his Word.

OBJECT LESSON—
FLAMING BIBLE
Needed: *Flaming Bible. A flaming Bible is an apparatus which looks like an authentic Bible. However, when it is opened, flames erupt from it.*
Sources: *One Way Street Store, 1-800-569-4537.*
Message: *The Bible is the most powerful, explosive book anywhere.*

As you hold up the Bible, say: **I'm holding in my hands the most powerful book ever written. Why is this book more special than Moby Dick or one of your comic books? The answer is because the very words written on each page were inspired by God. Although, he, himself, did not write the sixty-six books in the Bible, it was by way of his Holy Spirit communicating to the writers' minds and hearts that God's message was conveyed.**

When you begin reading God's Word, you will soon discover that in many ways it is a love letter written to you. Yes, that sounds funny, but it's true! Through those sixty-six books, God shares with you the history of sinful man and the redemption God brought to us through the death and resurrection of his Son, Jesus.

The Bible is the only book that can help you deal with the sin in your life. It offers its readers hope, love, and a way to salvation. That is explosive! *Open the Flaming Bible causing it to flame.*

ACTIVITY—
MAKING A BOOK
Distribute 3x5 cards and pencils. Have kids fold the cards like a book. Instruct the children that you want them to be authors of one-sentence books. Pretend that their books will be published worldwide. Billions of people will see the books. They may write whatever sentence they wish, but it may be only one sentence! Have the kids title the front of their books. Allow the children to share their messages.

MATERNITY WARD

Focus: *You must be born again.*
Scripture: *John 3:1-8*

READY!

Make arrangements to take your group to a local hospital to visit the maternity ward. What better setting to discuss what it means to be born again.

Depending on the size of your group, you may be allowed to hold your lesson in a birthing room full of all the medical instruments and machines used in delivering a child. If the birthing room is not an option, then find a waiting room, conference room, or cafeteria to teach your lesson.

SET!

Make arrangements with a local hospital to visit their maternity ward. See if it will be possible for all the children to wear authentic scrubs like a doctor or nurse. Make sure your tour will be led by a health care professional who can answer any question about the birth of a child. This will be especially important as your group spends plenty of time observing the newborns. Be careful not to allow this time to become a lesson on sex education. That is not the focus or intent.

You can create excitement about this lesson by offering a prize to the child who dresses most like a doctor, nurse, or baby.

GO!

Visit the maternity ward. As your group tours the hospital, encourage them to ask appropriate questions about what happens during childbirth.

1. **How long is the typical pregnancy?**
2. **How big is the average baby?**
3. **How long does it take to deliver a baby?**
4. **Who is usually involved in a typical delivery?**

What Does God Say?

Familiarize yourself with the Scripture found in John 3:1-8 and then share it with your group. This is the story of Jesus when he told Nicodemus, "You must be born again."

Do the object lesson. After the object lesson, distribute a 3x5 card and pencil to each student. Ask the kids to write down the answers to the following questions:

1. **Today we have seen babies who are less than one day old. What will it take for them to someday become born again?**

2. **What kind of change occurs in the life of the person who is newly born again?**

3. **What happens to the person who is never born again?**

4. **Are you born again?**

Wrap Up

To close the session, have your kids gather in a huddle to pray. Ask the group if there is anyone present who wants to be changed by God and be born again.

Award the prize to the winner of the contest.

OBJECT LESSON

Needed: A piece of thick construction paper, a fairly light paperweight, and two thick books.

Set Up: On a table or tray place the two books about six inches apart.

Message: You must be born again.

Say: **Let's imagine that we need to build a bridge between these two books. The problem is that we only have a single sheet of paper from which to construct the bridge. Let's test it. I'll lay the piece of paper as a bridge between the two books. Now I'll place the paperweight on the bridge and see what happens. My bridge sags when the weight is placed on it. I guess my bridge is no good!**

Before we throw my bridge into the trash, let's see if it can be changed so that it will be a much stronger bridge. Maybe if I fold it a few times it will make a difference. (Fold the paper into a fan using half-inch folds.) **Now that my bridge has been changed, let's see if it is strong enough to hold my paperweight.** (Carefully place the paper weight in the center of the bridge. It should not sag!)

Wow! My new bridge is now strong enough to support the paperweight. With a simple change, my bridge, which was once useless is now strong and useful.

You and I can be useful to God if we, too, are changed. When we offer ourselves to him, he will mold, fold, and makes us into new people, strong people of faith. That is what it means to be born again.

NEWSPAPER PLANT

Focus: *Share God's message.*
Scripture: *Mark 16:15*

READY!

The local newspaper plant is a marvelous setting for a lesson on spreading the good news of Jesus Christ. It is amazing how a single press can produce thousands of newspapers which are delivered to homes and businesses throughout an area.

God calls us to be deliverers of news, also. His Word clearly teaches that his message of hope, love, and salvation is to be delivered by his people. His people are to share their testimonies by witnessing to the lost souls of their community.

SET!

Arrange for a tour of the local newspaper plant. Make sure the children will be able to see the entire publication process. Have the tour guide point out the scanners, radios, and televisions in the news room that tip off reporters to breaking news. Be sure to see the process of getting the story from the reporter to the editor to layout to the presses and to the public.

GO!

Tour the newspaper plant. See how the newspaper is produced from start to finish. Ask to specifically see as many of these areas of the plant as possible: press

room, mailroom, plate room, guild, and layout room.
Allow the children to ask questions from the tour
guide. You may also ask these:

1. **How many newspapers are printed each day?**
2. **How much paper and ink are used each day?**
3. **What happens if a press breaks down?**
4. **How many people does it take to produce a newspaper?**
5. **How do you use recycled newspaper?**
6. **What is the oldest newspaper plant in the United States?**

After your tour is completed, gather your group into
a general meeting area. If no area is available, ask to
use the employee cafeteria.

What Does God Say?

Say: **Before Jesus ascended into Heaven, he told his
disciples something very important. Let's take a look
at Mark 16:15. There Jesus said, "Go everywhere in the
world. Tell the Good News to everyone" (ICB).**

**That verse proves that God wants us to tell our lost
friends about Jesus! Some people don't know how to
do that. So, for the next few minutes we're going to
practice.** Do the object lesson and then the activity to
have kids practice telling others.

Wrap Up

Close in a circle of prayer. Pray that God will empower
each child to be bold in sharing their faith. Also, allow
children to pray aloud for their lost loved ones.

OBJECT LESSON
Needed: An 8x8 sheet of flash paper (available from most magic shops); a match; a felt-tip pen.
Say: *I want you to watch as I write a letter to a friend of mine. (Begin writing.) This friend is a very nice person. She is very talented. A lot of people like her, and she always seems to be doing nice things for people who are less fortunate.*

The problem with my friend is that she is not a Christian. That means that she does not follow Jesus nor has she asked him to forgive her of her sins.

I'm writing this letter because I want my friend to know how much I want her to follow God. I'm also explaining that Jesus died on the cross to forgive her sins. I'm glad God has given me the opportunity to lead this person to his Son.

My friend is very smart. I know that after she reads my letter, she'll do the right thing. I'm sure she will begin to follow Jesus.

There! My letter is complete! It's ready to be mailed.

But wait! (Take your lighter or match.) *Many people out there in the world are God-loving Christians, but they never share the good news. They never make an attempt to lead someone closer to Jesus. Isn't that sad? It's almost as though they don't care.* (Light paper. It will flash and disappear.)

Remember, God wants us to be his witness. He has called us to tell others about him.

ACTIVITY
Give each child a piece of newsprint and a pencil. Instruct the children to write a letter to a lost friend or loved one. The purpose is to share their faith and testimony in hopes of leading someone to Jesus. In the letter, have the children include these elements:
1. Greeting
2. Description of tonight's lesson
3. Concern for their spiritual life
4. Urgency to follow Jesus
5. Closing that states you will be praying for them.

You can simplify these steps depending on the age of the children in your group. Adults may need to assist some children.

POLICE TRAINING ACADEMY

Focus: *Watch out for the enemy.*
Scripture: *1 Peter 5:8, 9; James 4:7, 8*

READY!

Teaching our kids to recognize the enemy is vital. A police training academy is an appropriate setting to facilitate such a lesson. Even our younger children understand the effects gangs and criminals have on our world. But in this setting you can help your kids realize they not only have enemies in this world, but also in the spiritual realm. With your help and the help of some trained police officers, you can aid in the protection of your children both spiritually and physically.

SET!

Arrange to have a tour of the local police academy. Be sure that the tour will include the classrooms, exercise and training rooms, and the target range. Try to arrange for a self-defense demonstration and a demonstration of an officer taking target practice.

GO!

Take a tour of the training facility. Ask for a demonstration of some basic self-defense techniques which could be used by the kids in the event they are ever mugged. Also, set up a demonstration of an officer taking target practice at the facility gun range. When the demonstrations have been completed, find a general meeting area where you may conduct the rest of your lesson. Ask an academy officer for an interview.

Give each child one 3x5 card and a pencil. Tell the children that they may write down and ask the officer any question which relates to his job.

1. Do most of the criminals you arrest have long police records?

2. How many criminals have you arrested?

3. What suggestions do you have for these kids to help keep them out of trouble?

4. How old are most criminals when they begin their life of crime?

5. What should these children do if one of their friends is beginning to do unlawful things such as stealing, taking drugs, or skipping school?

After the interview, do the object lesson.

Wrap Up

Gather your students in a circle, holding hands. Have a volunteer pray that each child present would continue to grow in Christ and would put their faith and trust in God. Also, pray that everyone in the group would remember to call upon the Lord when the enemy, the devil, comes and tempts them to disobey God.

OBJECT LESSON

Needed: *a telephone (preferably a fake phone which has the ability to ring)*

Message: *When you are confronted with the enemy, it is important to call upon God for help.*

Make your phone ring and pretend you are talking with someone. After a minute or so, hang up and say: **Today we have been talking mostly about enemies in our cities, jails, and schools. But God's Word tells us that there is another enemy about whom we need to be very concerned. The fiercest, sneakiest, most dangerous of all enemies is the devil himself. He will stop at nothing to ruin our lives. He tempts us to lie, cheat, and steal. In fact, until you learn how to defend yourself, you will lose to him every time. Here is a list of things you should do when the devil comes your way:**

1. 1 Peter 5:8 says, "Control yourselves and be careful! The devil is your enemy. And he goes around like a roaring lion looking for someone to eat" (ICB). It is important to always be ready for one of the devil's attacks. He is always looking for ways to tempt us to disobey God. So be on the lookout!

2. 1 Peter 5:9 says, "Refuse to give in to the devil. Stand strong in your faith" (ICB). It is vital to never give in to the devil. If you give him an inch, he will take a mile.

3. James 4:7, 8 says, "Give yourselves to God. Stand against the devil, and the devil will run away from you. Come near to God, and God will come near to you" (ICB). Submitting yourself to God is the best defense against the devil. The devil hates it when we put our trust in the Lord, and the devil will take off when he knows you are coming close to God.

4. Stay in touch! What a luxury it is to know we can call on God at any time and from anywhere. With this telephone *(hold it up),* **I may have a bad connection or may even get disconnected, but rest assured that when you call on God, he will come to your aid without delay!**

BASEBALL DIAMOND

Focus: *Jesus is the best trophy.*
Scripture: *Matthew 25:21*

READY!

Baseball is as American as apple pie. In fact, it is referred to as the great American pastime. Millions of people and many generations have been captivated by this sport. Many children and adults either participate in or are spectators of baseball.

The greatest reward for a baseball player is to win a game by hitting a home run over the fence. As the hitter rounds third base and heads for home plate, the fans in the stands rise to their feet and cheer. Teammates give congratulations through pats on the back and high fives.

In the life of a Christian, there may be many rewards along the way, but the greatest reward we can receive is the praise from Jesus when we have rounded all the bases and have headed for "home plate"—Heaven! Use this lesson to drive home the point that the praise given to us by Jesus will be our greatest reward.

SET!

Arrange for a tour at a professional ballpark. Minor league parks can also be found in many cities throughout the United States. If no professional facility is available, local colleges, universities, or even high schools have well-groomed ball diamonds and locker rooms.

Arrange a tour of the stadium or park. If there is a Christian player on the team, he may be willing to help with the tour and sign autographs at the end.

Conclude your lesson by teaching on the field. Make sure the children are allowed to run the bases, one at a time. Have the children sit near or around the pitcher's mound.

GO!

Visit all the areas of the ballpark, ending up on the field for the lesson.

Say: **Did you pretend to hit a game-winning home run? How did it feel? As you ran around the bases, did you sense the excitement you might really feel if you hit a home run?**

What Does God Say?

Say: **In Matthew 25, the story is told of man who was going away on a trip. He had lots of money, so he gave $5,000 to one of his workers to invest for him while he was away. He gave $2,000 to another worker and $1,000 to another worker. While he was gone, the one with $5,000 invested it wisely and earned another $5,000. Also, the one with $2,000 invested the money wisely and earned another $2,000. But the man with $1,000 dug a hole in the ground and buried the money for safekeeping.**

After a long time, the man returned from his trip. He went to his workers to find out how well they had done with the money he had entrusted to them

Who do you think deserved a reward when the boss returned? Two of the workers doubled the money, but one did nothing but hide it. The boss was very pleased with the ones who worked hard, but he

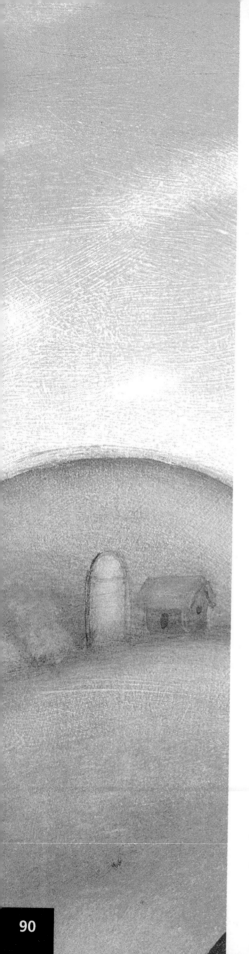

was very displeased with the one who did nothing. Let me read to you what the boss said to the workers who worked hard:

"You did well. You are a good servant who can be trusted. You did well with small things. So I will let you care for much greater things. Come and share my happiness with me" (Matthew 25:21, ICB).

In other words, the boss gave his two successful workers big promotions. If we read further, we find out that the third worker was fired, thrown out! All three workers knew what their boss expected, and even though each was given a different amount, they all knew that the boss expected them to put the money to good use, to make more money. Nothing more was expected of any one worker; they all had exactly the same responsibility. The problem occured when the third worker was too fearful of losing what he was given rather than doing what was expected.

Each of us is given different talents, skills, or abilities, and we all have different roles which we are responsible to fulfill. However, we are all equally expected to do God's will with what we have been given. Doing the right things and pleasing Jesus is not always easy. All he asks that we do is our best, and he tells us he will help us.

Yes, it's great to hit home runs and to win trophies and to achieve the acclaim of others, but let's remember the greatest reward. It is knowing that we are doing our best to please Christ.

Do the object lesson.

Wrap Up

Gather the children in a circle around home plate.

Say: **One day we will all round third base and head**

for "home"—Heaven. It is a reality that we will one day leave this body for a spiritual body. We will go to another home. Let's pray that we do our very best in pleasing Jesus so that one day, when we stand at Heaven's gates, Jesus will say to us, "Well done, good and faithful servant . . . come and share in your Master's happiness."

Close in a circle of prayer.

TENNIS COURT

MUST SEES
- Practice courts
- Regulation play courts
- Serving machine

SNACK
Apple

Focus: *Don't go out of bounds.*
Scripture: *Psalm 37:27*

READY!

The Bible clearly teaches that Christians must be very careful not to get off the straight and narrow path which God has laid out for us. It is God's desire that we resist the devil and set our eyes completely on him.

An excursion to a neighborhood tennis court will supply the right scene for a lesson on "not going out of bounds." Here you will be able to teach that it takes discipline and practice to keep a tennis ball in play. In the same way, you will also be able to share how important it is to keep your spiritual life going in the right direction.

MUST HAVES
- Rackets
- Balls
- Green apple
- Tennis rule book

TO-DO LIST
- Arrange for a tennis instructor to give a demonstration and some pointers.

SET!

Reserve a local tennis court prior to your arrival. If at all possible, line up a tennis instructor from a tennis club or school to meet your group. Have each child bring a tennis racket and you can supply the balls.

GO!

Once at the court, spread the children out and begin allowing the children to hit the ball back and forth to each other. If there are numerous courts, spread the children out even more. At this point, do not worry about the rules. Instead, you want to give the children the opportunity to get the feel for the racket and making contact with the ball.

After a short while, line all the children up on one side of the court and allow them to take turns serving the ball. Have your tennis instructor give a short lesson on how this is done. You may also now want him to explain the basic rules of the game. It is important that he strongly emphasize the significance of keeping your ball in play and not letting it sail out of bounds.

If time permits, have the children sit on the side and watch as you and three other players demonstrate a game of doubles tennis. You may wish to use only adults for this exercise.

After the game has been played, gather the children on one side of the court for the object lesson.

What Does God Say?

After the object lesson, say: **Let's see if you can guess which Bible story I was talking about earlier.** (Hold up the apple.) **Who went out of bounds when they ate the fruit from the tree of the knowledge of good and evil? Right! Adam and Eve!**

Summarize the complete story found in Genesis 3.

It is important to know that Adam and Eve didn't think it was a big deal to go out of bounds and sin against God's Word. They didn't think taking one small bite of a piece of fruit would change their lives forever. But, boy, were they wrong! Because of that one act of disobedience, they would:

1. **be thrown out of the Garden of Eden**
2. **have to grow their own food**
3. **have pain when giving birth**
4. **grow old and die.**

Wrap Up

Gather in a circle. Close by challenging your children with the verse from Psalm 37:27: "Turn from evil and do good; then you will dwell in the land forever" (NIV). Say: **I encourage you not to go out of bounds. Stay close to God, following his will for your life, and you will never see yourself separated from him.**

OBJECT LESSON
Needed: Bible, tennis ball, green apple
Set Up: none

Hold up the apple and tennis ball for all to see. Ask these questions: **What do these things have in common? Also, what Bible story would go along with these two objects?**

Some children may answer: both objects are round; both objects are green; both objects cost money. The children may or may not guess that the fall of Adam and Eve is the story in the Bible you are looking for and that the fruit represents good and evil.

Say: **Yes, your answers are all right, but there is one similarity between these objects that we have overlooked.**

Maybe a short lesson on the rules of tennis may help.

Again, demonstrate how to hit a serve. Show proper form as well as display where you must stand in order to serve the ball. Instruct the children on the importance that the serve land in the box or square on the other side of the net. Hit a few serves. Some should be clearly in play while others should be out. After this is done, gather the children in the box you just served in.

Say: **Some of my serves were right down the middle and clearly in the box. Others, though, were out of bounds. They missed the box completely. But let me ask you this. If a serve is only out by a few inches, is it really out? Do you think the judges will let it slide? No! You are right. If a ball is out of bounds even a little bit, it is officially out. The best and surest way of playing tennis is to hit the ball so that it is clearly in bounds.**

AIRPORT SECURITY

MUST SEES
- Surveillance camera monitors
- Luggage check area
- Passenger check area
- Security office

SNACK
Black licorice (symbolizes the darkness of sin) or Hershey Kisses (see if the machine can detect this)

MUST HAVES
- Several small, handheld video games or pagers labeled "sin"
- A cross made from craft sticks
- A large nail or spike

TO-DO LIST
- Arrange to see behind-the-scenes security activities.
- Alert tour guide to your object lesson of planting small electronic devices on a few children before they go through the metal detector.

Focus: *You sins will find you out!*
Scripture: *Numbers 32:23; Genesis 3*

READY!

Have you ever flown on an airplane before? It's a lot of fun! But airports have to be protective of the people they serve. It is the number one priority for them to be sure everyone is safe. But safe from whom? Terrorists.

With terrorism on the rise, airport security has been improved steadily worldwide. The most obvious sign of this security is the walk-through metal detectors. They can detect keys, weapons, and even heart pacemakers. They monitor what is taken onto the aircraft.

The metal detector can be used to illustrate the lesson that no matter how tiny the sin a person may be hiding, God knows about it. We may think it insignificant, but God will hold us accountable.

SET!

Arrange to take a tour of the airport security area. Ask to see the surveillance cameras that monitor the parking lots and concourses. Also, ask to be allowed to view the area where luggage is checked and suspicious looking packages are detonated.

Get permission from airport security to allow each child to walk through the metal detector. You should tip off the guard that you have planted some small electronic devices on some of the children for an object lesson.

Prior to the meeting, glue two craft sticks together to make a cross. Also, find a large nail or spike.

GO!

Tour the various areas which are monitored by airport security personnel. When you get to the metal detectors, do the object lesson.

What Does God Say?

Say: **The Bible clearly teaches that even the smallest sins will be brought to light. Eventually, the sinner will be caught. In fact the Bible says so in Numbers 32:23, "Know for sure that you will be punished for your sin" (ICB).**

Many boys and girls think that they can disobey their parents, cheat on tests and homework, lie, or steal without ever getting caught. The Bible says this just isn't so.

Ask the children to help you list people in the Bible whose sins caught up with them (Adam and Eve, Moses, Lot's wife, David, Judas, Peter, Paul, and Ananias and Sapphira). Next, retell the biblical account of the fall of man found in Genesis 3. Make sure to stress the fact that Adam and Eve thought that their sin would not catch up with them. Three key verses help demonstrate the thoughts one may have when contemplating and engaging in sin. If time permits, study these verses with your group.

1. Genesis 3:4: "You will not die." Notice how Adam and Eve were tricked.

2. Genesis 3:6: Eve enticed Adam. Notice how Eve thought she got away with the sin.

3. Genesis 3:21: Their attempt to cover themselves was inadequate. Notice how God had to cover their nakedness.

Wrap Up

Pass around the cross you made and the large nail so the children can touch them. As they are making their way through the group, close the session by sharing how Jesus died a terrible death on a cross for our sins.

Close in a circle of prayer. Allow the children time to ask for his forgiveness and victory over sins.

OBJECT LESSON
Needed: *a few small handheld video games or pagers*
Set Up: *Write the word "sin" on a piece of masking tape and adhere it to the objects. Prior to arriving at the airport, plant a pager or hand-held video game on five children. Ask them not to tell anyone that they have these objects in their pockets.*
Message: *You can't hide your sins from God.*

When you get to the metal detector, have everyone empty their pockets of all the coins, keys, and remove their metal belts (except for the five children with the objects).

Say: **The metal detector will judge the properties of your body and your clothes to see if you have any metal on you. This machine is used to detect bombs and guns. When a person who has a gun or bomb enters the metal detector, the machine will signal a warning.**

Now that each of you has emptied your pockets of metals, such as keys, coins, belts with metal buckles, and jewelry, you should now be able to pass through the metal detector without setting off the alarm. So, one by one, I want you to pass through the machine. I also want you to know that five children have been planted with an object which will probably set off the alarm. As these children walk through, notice that the object they are hiding is not visible.

As the children go through the metal detector, the ones with the objects will be detected. After everyone has walked through, gather the children in a pre-arranged area, perhaps an empty concourse.

HIGH

SCHOOL

Focus: *Keep God's commandments in your heart.*
Scripture: *Psalm 119:11*

READY!

In the 1962 decision in *Engle v. Vitale*, the U.S. Supreme Court struck down the practice of school sponsored prayers. The justices who wrote opinions in favor of the decision made it clear that while children who did not wish to participate in the prayers could abstain or leave the room, there was still an appearance of establishment of religion, something that the First Amendment of the Constitution of the United States prohibits.

Now, public schools have become open battlegrounds for spiritual warfare. While most children experience their own spiritual struggles in private, children who are developing their faith and who want to express their faith find themselves battling in the open at their own school.

This excursion takes your children down the halls and corridors of a public school. Here they will discuss the effects of the separation of church and state. Use this lesson to reinforce the truth that no matter what opposition children may face, God will always be with them.

SET!

I think you will be surprised at how easy it is to schedule this field trip in a public school. It is important to remember to try to go to the school after hours so as not to stir up controversy. Make arrangements to see all the different areas of the school that the kids will someday use when they attend the school. Get permission to have your lesson in the library.

GO!

Tour your local high school. Show your group the classrooms, library, cafeteria, and gym. All these areas will impress your children as they realize that one day they will probably attend a school similar in size and structure.

Prior to the tour, give to each child a 3x5 card and a pencil. Ask your children to list things in the school which you might also find in a church. Also, have them list things that are missing in the school that would probably be found in the church.

After the tour has been completed, gather in the library for the lesson. Begin by asking the children to share the information on their 3x5 card. Ask:

1. What things did you find in the school which can also be found in the church? (Furniture, windows, classrooms, books, etc.)

2. What things did you find missing in the school which would probably be found in church? (Choir robes, pictures of Jesus, a Cross, the Ten Commandments.)

3. What things happen in your school that show that people do not follow God's will? (Vandalism, cheating, lying, fighting)

Say: **Today during our tour of the public high school, you may have noticed that there was nothing religious in the building. Why do you think that is?**

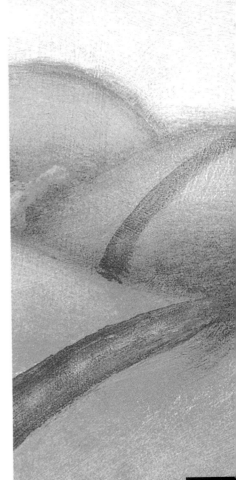

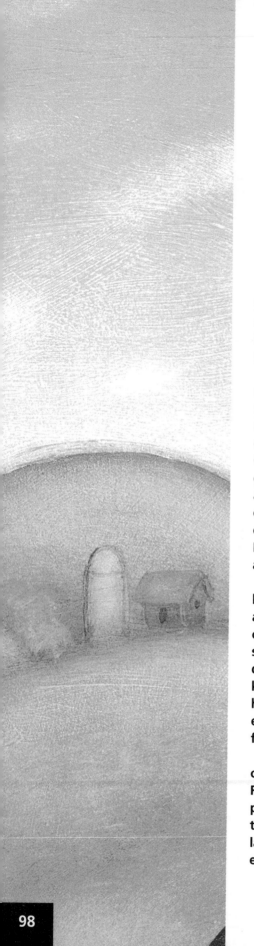

At one time, many public schools led their students in public prayer, asking God to direct and bless the students, the teachers, the parents, and the country. In 1962, the United States Supreme Court decided to prohibit public schools from leading public prayers.

Unfortunately, many people have taken this decision to an extreme. This court decision has prompted many non-Christian and even anti-Christian people and groups to attempt to strip out any and all references and acknowledgements even to the existence of God. Many schools no longer have Christmas programs or Easter breaks. Teachers who believe in God are forbidden to share their faith or teach that God created the heavens and the earth. Some schools have even prohibited students from forming their own Bible study groups, though this has been challenged and overturned in recent court decisions.

But that's not the worst part. Now, because it has become unpopular to claim to be a Christian at school and because schools are afraid to teach morals based on God's Word, Christian values are disappearing from schools. We read about kids drinking and taking drugs, kids having babies, kids bringing guns and knives to school, and kids killing other kids. You see how some kids disrespect their teachers, school property, and other kids. This is all because people do not follow God's will.

This is why it is so important for Christian kids to be open about their faith in God and their walk with Jesus. Regardless of what people say the law says or what people say the Constitution says, when Christian kids go to school, God goes to school. Besides, no matter what laws we pass and who stands guard at the door, God is everywhere. Nobody can keep God out of school.

Do the object lesson.

What Does God Say?

Say: **There are many examples of people in the Bible who stood up for their faith. Moses, Daniel, Shadrach, Meschach, Abednego, and Paul are just a few. They all lived by the simple truth found in Psalm 119:11 which says, "I have taken your words to heart so that I would not sin against you" (ICB). They all knew that their decision to stand up for God would not be popular or easy—all of our examples faced death because of it. But they also knew that without God's Word and truth guiding them, they would be easy prey for the devil, which would be worse than death.**

Wrap Up

Say: **You may see some bad things happening at your school. Cheating, fighting, drugs, and vandalism are just a few examples. But today, let's begin to pray that God will help each of us be faithful when people make fun of our beliefs. Let's pray that God will help us to live our faith openly so that other people will want to become Christians. Then we will be able to change our schools and then our society for Christ.**

Close in a circle of prayer.

OBJECT LESSON

Needed: two 4" x 11" pieces of paper and rubber cement

Set Up: Write "Remove God from schools" on one piece of paper. On the back of that piece, place a 2" dab of rubber cement near the right corner. Write "you can't remove God from schools" on the other piece of paper and fold the words inside until it is a small square. Stick the folded paper on the back of the other piece in the dab of rubber cement.

Message: Although people have attempted to remove God from school, when God is in the hearts of students, he is abundantly present.

Hold the paper so that the kids can read the words "remove God from schools."

Tear off narrow strips of paper and hold them against the folded paper. When you finish tearing the paper, you should have all the strips held against the folded paper.

Fold the torn strips so that they clump together and stick to the rubber cement.

As you unfold the folded paper so the kids can see the words "you can't remove God from schools," explain that whenever Christian kids go to school, God goes there, too! The folded strips will be on the back of the paper, out of the children's sight.

ART GALLERY

MUST SEES
- Famous artist exhibits
- Restoration rooms
- Archives

SNACK
Fortune cookies (because the statements in the fortune cookie are usually inaccurate, they are symbolic of the idea that no one really knows your future but God)

MUST HAVES
- Paper
- Paint
- A black marker
- Crayons

TO-DO LIST
- Arrange to have available at least one painting the children can touch.
- Arrange for a painting demonstration.
- Make sure the tour will not include inappropriate material for your group.

ACTIVITY
Give each child a sheet of paper and a crayon.
Say: **The artist has in his mind a plan to show how the painting will turn out. God also has a plan for you. Draw a picture of what God is planning for your future or draw a picture of what you want to become.**

Focus: *Follow God's plan for your life.*
Scripture: *Jeremiah 29:11*

READY!

God has a plan for each of our lives. Sometimes, however, we don't understand that plan when God allows circumstances, tragedy, problems, or illness to enter our world. Just as a painter has a vision, plan, and idea working as he puts paint onto a canvas, God has a vision, plan, and idea as he patiently molds us into his work of art. Planning a visit to an art gallery or studio where artwork is created is an appropriate atmosphere to raise the question, "What is God's plan for your life?"

SET!

Arrange for a tour of a local art gallery or a college where art is taught—most colleges also have art galleries to exhibit donated artwork, whether they teach art or not. You should make sure that the tour will not include pieces which may be objectionable or inappropriate for your age group.

Art galleries or studios usually have hundreds of paintings in their possession. See if the gallery can make several available for your children to inspect. Be sure to get permission or arrange to have available at least one finished painting that the children can touch to feel the brushstrokes and smell the paint.

GO!

As you tour the gallery, help the children realize the enormous amount of time it takes to produce a professional painting. Have each one touch the canvas where the brush strokes may be felt. Attempt to smell the paint that has soaked and dried into the heavy, durable material. When that has been completed, gather the children into a general area where the canvasses are placed to be painted. Set up a painting demonstration and an interview with an artist and use the questions listed below or any other questions the children may have.

1. **How long does it take to complete a painting?**

2. **What materials are used?**

3. **Where do you get the image you paint? Do you use a picture or is it in your imagination?**

4. **What is the largest painting you have done?**

5. **What happens when you make a mistake? Do you start over or do you use the flawed painting?**

After the demonstration, do the object lesson. After the object lesson, have the children do the activity.

Wrap Up

Show off some of the pictures and allow children to add commentary to their own masterpieces. Be sure to add that we are all "paintings in progress" and that God is never done with us. Close in a circle of prayer.

BEAUTY SALON

Focus: *God looks at the inside.*
Scripture: *1 Samuel 16:7*

READY!

The Bible says that Christians should not worry about
what we wear or eat because God takes care of us. If
that is true, why do so many people spend so much of
their money on making themselves look better?
Billions of dollars are spent each year on designer
clothes, fat-reducing surgical procedures, cosmetics,
and fancy hairdos. In fact there are many magazines
on the news stands advocating that you spend your
time and money becoming more beautiful. *Glamour*,
Mademoiselle, and *Self* are just a few examples.

A trip to a beauty salon is an appropriate setting for
a lesson on the difference between inner beauty and
outer beauty.

SET!

Make arrangements to tour a local beauty salon. To
get a bigger impact, you might want to check out a
"day spa" where people go to get haircuts, manicures,
pedicures, facials, herbal wraps—a full day of complete
pampering.

Prior to arriving, set up with the management of the
salon that two or three of the children would receive a
buzz haircut (where almost all the hair is cut off). Be
sure to get written parental approval.

GO!

Tour a local beauty salon. The national chains usually have more floor space and would probably be better suited to handle a larger group.

After the tour, present the kids who will be getting the buzz haircuts. Before the children's hair is cut, ask the other children what they like best about each child who is going to receive the buzz. They may answer such things as "fun," "crazy," "loving," etc.

Also, before the children receive their buzz, ask them to share with the class how important they think their hair is to them. Ask them to explain why nice clothes and the newest, coolest shoes make them feel good about themselves.

After the haircuts, ask the children if their friends have really changed even though their appearances have. Then ask the kids who got the haircuts if they feel they have changed.

Do the object lesson.

What Does God Say?

Say: **The Bible says, "God does not see the same way people see. People look at the outside of a person, but the Lord looks at the heart" (1 Samuel 16:7, ICB).**

Beauty is really found on the inside of a person. You may think that the outward apparel, like shoes, clothes, and hair styles, is what is important, but it's not. God knows that our looks will change over time, but with him on the inside, we will always have beauty.

Wrap Up

Close by having each child look into a handheld mirror. The prayer that follows should thank God for loving us inside and out. (It would be a good idea to have a nice T-shirt in reserve for the child who got the package with the ratty, old one.) Close in a circle of prayer.

OBJECT LESSON

Needed: two identical gift boxes; a nice, new T-shirt and a ratty, old T-shirt; and wrapping paper

Set Up: Prior to going to the beauty salon, place each shirt in a box. Wrap the box with the dirty, torn T-shirt with the finest wrapping paper you can find. Wrap the other box similarly, but proceed to get the box dirty and smash it up so that it looks worn.

Message: What is on the outside does not always reflect what is on the inside.

Before leaving for the beauty salon, offer the boxes to the two children whose birthdays were most recent. Let them choose their packages and then proceed to take the packages with them (unopened) to the salon.

After the haircuts have been given to the other children, ask the two children with the boxes to come forward. Have the children enthusiastically open their boxes as though it is Christmas morning. The child with the dirty box will produce a new shirt. The child with the nice package will produce an old, ruined shirt.

Say: As you can see by this lesson, what is on the outside does not always reflect what is on the inside. You would have thought that the pretty package would have produced a pretty gift, but that just wasn't so.

ARMY NATIONAL GUARD

MUST SEES
- Military vehicles
- Equipment
- Weapons
- Uniforms
- Soldier's gear

SNACK
Rock candy (symbolic of David's smooth stone)

Focus: *Faith defeats the giants in your life.*

Scripture: *1 Samuel 17:20-58*

MUST HAVES
- Carman's Yo Kids CD and a means for playing it
- A small, smooth stone

TO-DO LIST
- Make sure the kids will be able to try on some of the uniforms or gear.

READY!

The Army National Guard is often dispatched when trouble arises and order needs to be restored. Does this remind you of a great story in the Old Testament? Of course! It's the story of David and Goliath. This is a favorite with children since David was a young boy and his bravery and faith in God resulted in Goliath and the Philistine army being defeated.

The Israelites were facing the mighty Philistines, and this was a battle that was about to become a catastrophe. Then a little shepherd boy stepped forward with nothing but a sling and one stone from his shepherd's bag. But David had become a crack shot having killed both lions and bears when they attacked his sheep.

It was a small child full of faith in God and a sling that were the ingredients needed to be victorious over Goliath and a whole army.

The Army National Guard sometimes uses heavy military equipment and weapons to secure a situation, but in our spiritual life it only takes faith in God to win the battle. This lesson will look at the kind of faith David had and the kind of faith we should have.

SET!

Make arrangements to have a tour of the local National Guard Amory. Make sure the kids will be able to see lots of heavy military equipment, including vehicles, weapons and other gear.

GO!

As you tour the Army National Guard facility, be prepared to have the children try on some military gear. They can experience what it's like to have a helmet on or to walk in heavy military boots. Have a heavy backpack for them to strap on their back. Help the children understand what David must have felt like having been asked to wear the King's heavy military armor. Truly, David had a better idea.

Do the object lesson.

What Does God Say?

Although no single verse is highlighted in this lesson, it is important for the teacher to have a firm grasp and understanding of the biblical account of the story of David and Goliath found in 1 Samuel 17:20-58. Emphasize the main points of the story:

1. David put on God's full armor, not man's. Saul was amazed when he saw that David was just a boy. Saul told David not to be ridiculous, that he would be fighting a giant who had been in the army since he was a boy. But David persisted and convinced Saul that he was equal to the task. Saul gave David his own armor, helmet, and sword, but the armor was so big and bulky that David couldn't move. So he took it

> **OBJECT LESSON**
> **Needed:** one small, smooth rock
> **Set Up:** none
> **Message:** God doesn't need powerful weapons to defeat our enemies.
>
> Hold up the rock and say: **Many times we think invading armies can only be stopped by using large planes, tanks, and ships. But look what God used to defeat an entire Philistine army: a small child and a small stone. But there was one thing that needed to be big. Of course, I am talking about David's faith. Without it, he would have been useless. But with faith, he was able to look that mean, old giant in the face and defeat both him and his comrades.**

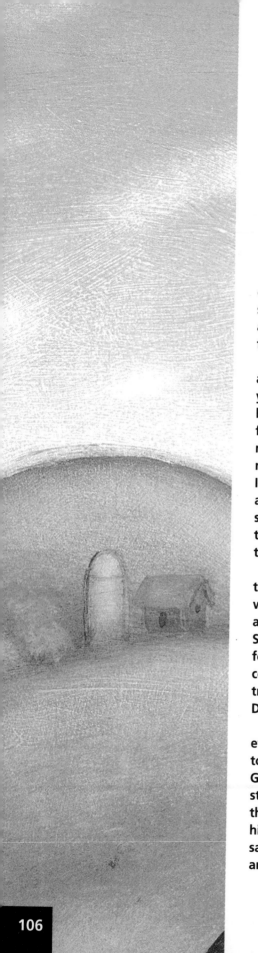

off. Then he picked up five smooth stones from the stream and put them in his shepherd's bag. Then, armed only with his shepherd's staff and sling, he faced Goliath, the giant.

2. Nowhere does the Bible say that David was afraid. Goliath was shocked and angry when he saw a young, red-cheeked boy. He began to threaten David by cursing him and shouting that he would feed his flesh to the birds and wild animals. But David showed no fear. David's voice rang out in return, "You come to me using a sword, a large spear and a small spear. But I come to you in the name of the Lord of heaven's armies. He's the God of the armies of Israel! You have spoken out against him. Today the Lord will give you to me" (1 Samuel 17:45, 46, ICB). This, again, proves that David had no fear!

3. He didn't let age get in his way. Goliath walked toward David and made fun of the little boy who would dare think he could defeat him. "Do you think I am a dog, that you come at me with a stick?" (1 Samuel 17:43, ICB). David's brothers had scolded him for being so foolish and told him that he was just a cocky brat and should return to his sheep. Saul had tried to discourage him from tackling the giant. But David was a boy with a mission.

4. David didn't take no for an answer. Even though everyone had said no to David, he went ahead. David took out one stone, put it in his sling and hurled it at Goliath. The rock hit the giant in the forehead. The stone sank in, and Goliath fell forward on his face to the ground. David took Goliath's own sword and killed him with it and then cut off his head. The Philistines saw that their champion was dead, and they turned and ran.

5. David knew who his commander was. David

decided to go into battle because Goliath and the Philistines cursed and defied the armies of the living God. He told Goliath, "Today the Lord will give you to me. I'll kill you, and I'll cut off your head. Today I'll feed the bodies of the Philistine soldiers to the birds of the air and the wild animals. Then all the world will know there is a God in Israel!" (1 Samuel 17:46, ICB). David knew that with God on his side the victory would be his!

Wrap Up

Say: Do you have some giant struggles in you life? Maybe some of you are hurting because your parents are divorced. Others may be dealing with a bully at school. Some of you could be having trouble getting good grades at school or making friends in your neighborhood. Whatever the case, remember that even though those problems may seem giant, with a lot of faith in God, He will see you through to victory.

Close by listening to the song "Sling, Bang, Boom" found on Carman's *Yo Kids* compact disc. In a unique way, it summarizes the events found in the David and Goliath story. Close in a circle of prayer.

ROAD SALT STORAGE FACILITY

MUST SEES
- Salt spreading vehicles
- Loading area
- Storage area

SNACK
Salted pretzels or salted potato chips

MUST HAVES
- Salt packets

TO-DO-LIST
- Gather enough salt packets for all the kids.
- Write "Matthew 5:13" on all the salt packets.

Focus: *Don't lose your saltiness.*
Scripture: *Matthew 5:13*

READY!

Mineral salt, which originally comes from sea water, has many uses. It has been used for countless things including as a seasoning and preservative for food. In Asia, it is a token and symbol of fidelity for those making a contract. In America it is used to melt ice on slippery highways. In the New Testament, Jesus made reference to the importance of salt as it symbolically relates to the life of a Christian.

Use this lesson to help kids understand their role as Christians in the world. Just as salt was used as a preservative, Christians should be able to help preserve good relationships and good behavior among their friends and even within their families. It isn't as though Christians can or should try to change others forcibly; their influence should be detected in another person's life after frequent and purposeful contact over time.

This lesson could easily be adapted to other settings, including the salt mines of the West or packaging plants where food is preserved. It could even be used around the dinner table where salty tasting foods could be sampled.

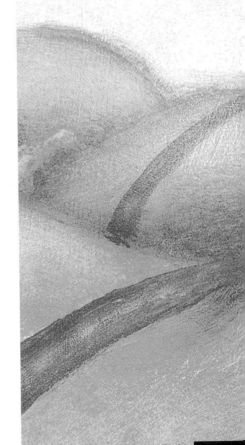

SET!

Most towns that experience any kind of cold weather conditions have road salt storage facilities to help combat the ice on the roads. Locate the nearest facility and schedule a tour. Find out whether the facility uses salt or other chemicals and additives in its road treament—you don't want kids touching or tasting some of these materials.

GO!

When taking the tour, ask to specifically see where the large amounts of salt are stored. You should check before you allow the children to touch, smell, or taste the salt, as many road crews do not use pure salt on roads; many use mixtures of various chemicals and abrasive materials to provide traction. Also, ask to see the great trucks which not only plow snow but also dispense salt onto the icy roads. Be sure to ask your tour guide to explain the process of how the salt melts the ice and snow. Also, allow your children to ask any pertinent questions they may have. When the tour has been completed, gather your group in a general meeting area for the rest of the lesson.

What Does God Say?

Say: **Did you know that God said you are salt? It's true! Hear what it says in Matthew 5:13: "You are the salt of the earth. But if the salt loses its salty taste, it cannot be made salty again. It is good for nothing. It must be thrown out for people to walk on" (ICB).**
   So far tonight, we have talked about how salt can

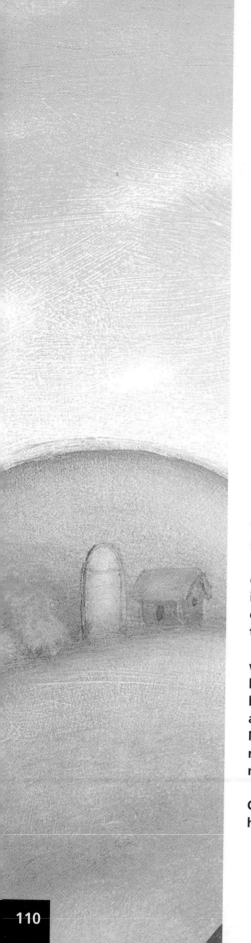

be used to melt ice and snow on the roads. In the New Testament and the ancient world, salt was used mostly as a preservative. It was used to keep things from going bad and to hold rotting at bay. Salt was packed into the carcass of slaughtered animals and was the only way to ensure freshness. So salt, then, preserved things from corruption. If a Christian is to be the salt of the earth, he must help those around him not to go bad or to rot!

We all have friends who, when we are around them, make it easy for us to be good. These may be some of your friends at church. But there are also certain people in whose company it is easy for us to let down our guard and become relaxed, even rotten. When around these people, it would be easy to do something dishonest or to tell a dirty story.

But Christians must be like salt. We must be the ones who keep situations clean and free from becoming rotten. We must be the people who, by our presence, defeat corruption and make it easier for others to be good.

We don't have to force people to act the way God wants all of us to act or believe the way we believe, but we should be actively telling our friends why we behave the way we do. They should see our actions and hear our speech and know that we are different. Many times they'll ask why, so we should also be ready and able to discuss how our friends can become more like Jesus.

So, are you salty? Do you make a real impact for Christ around your friends? Let's pray that God will help you become the salt he has called you to be.

Do the "Taste Test" object lesson.

Wrap Up

Give each child a small packet of salt available from most restaurants. On the front of the packet you will have written "Matthew 5:13" which is the key Scripture reference for the lesson.

Read the verse aloud again. Say: **I challenge you to keep this salt packet in your book bag, pants pocket, or someplace where you will see it often this week. Let it be a reminder to you that God expects you to be salty for him. The questions is, will you obey his Word and do just that?**

Close in a circle of prayer.

OBJECT LESSON—
TASTE TEST
Needed: *salted and unsalted potato chips, pretzels, and peanuts*
Set Up: *none*
Message: *Salt can make a difference.*

Allow the children to randomly taste a sample of both the salted and unsalted products. Then let them comment on the preference as to which type they most enjoyed. Many of the children will comment on how bland and strange the unsalted products tasted.

Say: **Most of us would agree that the foods without the salt seemed to be missing something. They just didn't have as much appeal as the salted products. Oh, the salted and unsalted peanuts, potato chips, and pretzels looked the same, but we know that they were not.**

CEMETERY

Focus: *What will they say about you
when you're gone?*
Scripture: *Hebrews 11:24-28;
Philippians 2:14, 15*

READY!

What will they say about you when you're gone?
That's the question you can ask during a lesson at a
cemetery. Some may think a cemetery is spooky. Others
will find it fun and exciting. Whatever the case, a
cemetery is the perfect place to talk about the impression we can leave after we've gone to be with Jesus.

SET!

Make arrangements to visit a cemetery. Make sure
either a caretaker or funeral director is present to
guide the kids through the steps of a funeral. Invite
parents to attend with their children. Make sure it will
be OK for the kids to make etchings of tombstones.

GO!

Begin with a brief tour of the cemetery. Have the caretaker show you any unique areas or buildings. Have
the caretaker explain a funeral in simple terms. Allow
the children to ask reasonable questions.
1. **How large is the cemetery?**
2. **How many plots are there?**
3. **How do you mow around all the headstones?**
4. **How long until the cemetery is full?**
Have children do the "Tombstone Search" activity.

What Does God Say?

Say: **Above all, God wants you to live a pure and blameless life. He says this plainly in Philippians 2:14, 15: "Do everything without complaining or arguing. Then you will be innocent and without anything wrong in you. You will be God's children without fault. But you are living with crooked and mean people all around you. Among them you shine like stars in the dark world" (ICB).**

Do you want your obituary to read that you were blameless and pure and that you shined for Jesus?

Some people's godly lives are remembered for thousands of years. Although the Bible is not an obituary, it does record the lives of many men and women. One man who made a real difference was Moses. He not only helped free the Hebrews from slavery in Egypt, but he also brought the Law of God down from Mt. Sinai.

Even after his death, his legacy of being a faithful, godly man lives on. It is recorded in Hebrews 11:24-28: "It was by faith that Moses, when he grew up, refused to be called the son of the king of Egypt's daughter. He chose to suffer with God's people instead of enjoying sin for a short time. He thought that it was better to suffer for the Christ than to have all the treasures of Egypt. He was looking only for God's reward. It was by faith that Moses left Egypt. He was not afraid of the king's anger. Moses continued strong as if he could see the God that no one can see. It was by faith that Moses prepared the Passover and spread the blood on the doors (ICB).

Obviously, Moses was remembered for his humility and faith in God. How will you be remembered?

Have kids do the "Writing an Obituary" activity.

Wrap Up

For this activity, you will need the caretaker's permission and one 11x17 piece of white paper and one crayon for each child. Instruct the children that they are going to produce grave etchings, the process where you lay a piece of paper over the writing on a headstone and color the paper. When you have colored the paper, you are left with an image of the headstone. Have adults assist the children.

Close in a circle of prayer.

OBJECT LESSON
Needed: a newspaper containing the obituary section
Message: We write our own obituary by the way we live.

Open the paper for the children to see. Say: *I'm holding an obituary. An obituary is the announcement of someone's death. It usually tells when a person was born, who their family was, where they worked, and what accomplishments they had in life. In a short paragraph, it tells who that person was. Let's read a few.* Read a few obituaries.

See, an obituary is an account of someone's life. Let me ask you a question. If you were to pass away today, what would you family and friends write in your obituary? Would they give account that you showed Jesus' love by helping others? Would they say that you loved learning about God and enjoyed going to church? Would they say how honest you were, that you had a lot of integrity? Would they say that you weren't selfish?

ACTIVITY—
WRITING AN OBITUARY
Pass out a 3x5 card and a pencil to each child. Have them write an obituary that includes their accomplishments and surviving family. Also, have them chronicle their faith journey.

When completed, say: **Moses left a history and legacy of being faithful. Above all, God wants you to be faithful, also. Will you be remembered as a person dedicated to God's call?**

THEATER STAGE

MUST SEES
- *Box office*
- *Stage*
- *Backstage*
- *Dressing rooms*
- *Lighting board*
- *Sound board*
- *Concessions area*

SNACK
Candy corn (it may look like corn; it may feel like corn; but once you taste candy corn, you know it's not genuine corn; it's an imitation)

MUST HAVES
- *Prizes for the game*
- *Copies of the optical illusions (figures A and B)*

TO-DO LIST
- *Get permission to use the stage for the game and lesson.*
- *Make copies of the illusions.*

Focus: *Be genuine!*
Scripture: *Matthew 7:15*

READY!

Everyone has seen either a play, a TV show, or a movie. In each of these, we see actors portraying other people, whether real or fictitious. Usually we view actors in light of the characters they portray. But we're often surprised when they do something in real life that we think is "out of character" or when they portray a character who is not like roles they've played in the past. It's easy to forget that the real-life actor is not necessarily like the character they portray.

It's the same with us. While most people claim to be Christians and while many attend church regularly, our society tells us that many people do not really live according to the faith they claim. Kids pick up on this quickly. If their parents, teachers, or other people they respect claim to believe one thing and do another, kids quickly learn the same behavior.

Use this lesson at the theater to emphasize the point that even when you pretend to be a Christian and fool some people, you can never fool God. This setting lends itself nicely to a lesson on what it means to be a "real Christian" and not one who simply acts like a believer when it's convenient to do so.

SET!

Many communities have a playhouse or theater. Most colleges and high schools have a theater or drama department with a stage. Make arrangements to have a tour of the theater. Try to get demonstrations of lighting effects, sound effects, and make-up effects.

GO!

Take a short tour of the theater facility. Be sure to ask specifically if you may see the dressing rooms, make-up area, box office, lighting and sound area, and concessions area. Ask for your tour guide to explain the function of each area. As you wind down the tour, be sure to end up on center stage with your group either sitting in front of you or sitting in the seats on the front row.

Have the children play the game. After the game, say: **There are a lot of people in the world who go to church, pray, tithe, sing in the choir, and go to Sunday school who never become Christians. They have never prayed for God to forgive their sins. They have never tried to stop sinning. They have never made him Lord of their lives. In a lot of ways they are actors acting like believers in Jesus Christ but without his Spirit working in their hearts.**

Here's a question for you: Are our five volunteers really monkeys, lions, horses, bumblebees, trees, cry babies, bulldozers, or airplanes? Or were they just acting like these things? Of course they were just acting! And so do the real actors who perform on this stage. They simply act. The roles they play are not real-life for them. It's pretend.

Sometimes we get tricked into thinking the actors on TV are real. Whether it be a cops-and-robbers show or a monster movie, sometimes the roles the actors play seem real.

> **GAME**
> Ask for five volunteers to come forward to center stage. Say: **Today we are in a theater where people learn to act and perform in plays. Here we are going to learn why it is important that we don't just act as Christians but that we live as genuine believers. But before we get started, I have brought up these wonderful volunteers to prove to you how easy it is to imitate something you are not. So without delay, I will tell these volunteers to act like something or someone. The child who acts or pretends the best will win a prize.** Show the children a prize of your choice.
> Have each of the children act like each of the following:
> - Monkey
> - Lion
> - Horse
> - Bumblebee
> - Tree
> - Cry baby
> - Bulldozer
> - Someone dying of hunger
> - Airplane

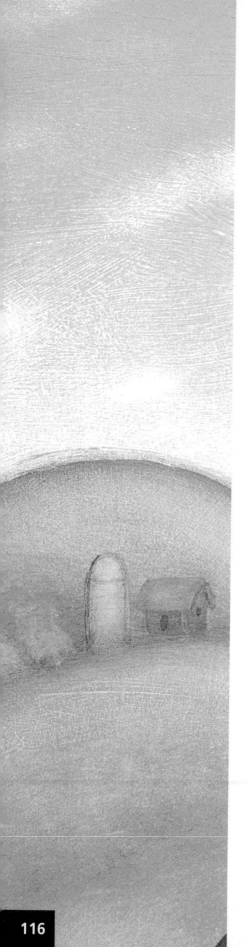

I want you to know that it is OK to pretend and use your imagination. Playing house or army is fun. But what is not good is to pretend to be a follower of Jesus when in reality, deep down in your heart, you know you are not being real. Jesus must forgive you of your sins and be Lord of your life for you to be a real Christian.

What Does God Say?

Say: What does God say about people who act like Christians but aren't? He says, "Beware!" Jesus proclaimed, "Be careful of false prophets. They come to you and look gentle like sheep. But they are really dangerous like wolves" (Matthew 7:15, ICB).

If you have ever laid your eyes on a sheep, it is easy to see that they are harmless. But we all know that wolves are dangerous and can cause serious harm. So can non-believers who claim to be godly! They can stir up a heap of trouble.

If you're acting like a follower of Jesus but you know you're not, then become a believer! If you are a believer but you're hanging around with someone at church or school who is beginning to get you into trouble, chances are they are like the wolves Jesus talked about. Beware!

Wrap Up

Gather in a circle of prayer. Spend some time praying for wisdom. Ask God to show the boys and girls who are the sheep and who are the wolves.

Figure A

Figure B

CITY HALL

Focus: *Follow the right leader.*
Scripture: *Daniel 6; Deuteronomy 13:4*

READY!

A trip to city hall has the perfect atmosphere to discuss how important it is to "follow your leaders." Elected officials are in office to help bring about a better community in which to live. They are also to protect the religious rights of those who follow God.

Use this lesson to unpack the turmoil Daniel found himself in when the government forbade him to worship the one, true God. Also, help apply this lesson by showing your children the process of justice.

SET!

Especially in smaller cities, it is possible to arrange a tour of city hall led by an elected official and possibly even the mayor. Ask that the tour include council chambers or wherever public meetings are held, public records, administrative offices, and the mayor's office.

GO!

Tour the various areas of the complex, being sure to allow the children the opportunity to ask questions at the various locations. After the tour, gather your group into a conference room, cafeteria, or other appropriate place to meet.

Do the object lesson and then ask the following questions:

1. **How many of you believe it is important to keep the laws of the land? Why?**

2. **What would you do if there were a new law that stated that you always had to wear a green shirt?**

3. **What would you do if there were a law that said you could not worship Jesus or God the Father anymore? And what if the law said that anyone worshiping him would be killed?**

What Does God Say?

Say: **That's what happened to the biblical character named Daniel. He was a godly man whose faith was put to the test.** Share the rest of the story from Daniel 6 and ask the children to respond to the following questions:

1. **What would you have done if you were Daniel? Would you have prayed anyway?**

2. **What are some ways we can be sure this doesn't happen in the city and county in which we live?** (Pray and vote.)

3. **What are some other biblical examples of people who stood up for their faith?** (Shadrach, Meshach, and Abednego; David; Jesus; and Paul)

4. **What are some examples of people today who have stood up for their faith?** (Missionaries)

Do the "Write a Law" activity.

Wrap Up

As a closing activity and if time permits, have fun playing the game "Follow the Leader." Let different children lead. Say: **Remember, it is important to follow the right leader. If the government ever tries to lead you astray, be bold and stand strong for God. He'll never let you down.**

Close by praying for your local, state, and national leaders.

OBJECT LESSON
Needed: Bible, one large sheet of large poster board, a marker
Set Up: none
Message: Rules help us direct our lives.
  Say: **Today we have learned that city hall is where ordinances and laws are made and where city officials direct the administration of a city government. It's a place where you go if you need a building permit to build a house. It's also the place where you pay fines for breaking the law. It's a place you can go to understand the laws and ordinances of the city.**
  How many of you have rules in your home? Most all of us have rules at home. "Do your homework before watching TV." "You must be in bed before 8:30 p.m. on school nights." "Don't cross the street without permission." *Write the kids' rules down on poster board.*
  Why do your parents have rules for you to live by? (Children should suggest that rules help keep you from harm and help you do what is right.) **Rules help us direct our lives. They help us understand our boundaries. Did you know that God's Word, the Bible** (hold up the Bible), **is our ultimate rule book? In fact, Deuteronomy 13:4 tells us that we must obey only God's commands and cling to him.**

ACTIVITY—
  WRITE A LAW
  Hand out a 3x5 card and pencil to each child. Allow the children to write a law which protects Christians' right to worship God. Their law may suggest that prayer in school be allowed. They may also write one which says people should not be forced to work on Sundays.

AUTO BODY SHOP

MUST SEES
- Tool area
- Welding equipment
- Paint area
- Frame straightener

SNACK
Nuts in the shell (to symbolize that there is something special under the "outside shell" of all of us)

Focus: *God doesn't want you to hurt.*
Scripture: *1 Peter 5:7*

READY!

Nothing hurts a new car owner worse than seeing his automobile wrecked in a collision. The upset owner can almost feel the pain himself as he sheepishly looks at the dented fender or the smashed front end. Fortunately, this type of damage can usually be repaired by trained auto body professionals.

However, there are other types of damages in life. These are the damages that harm people emotionally. They can cause depression or feelings of rejection, loneliness, or even anger. Oftentimes people keep these hurts inside where no one can see them, "inside hurts." You can't see these damages like the dings, scratches, and dents visible on a car. Even so, they are as equally painful to the victim of emotional damage as the victim of automobile damage.

Scheduling a tour of a collision repair shop will help your children understand the differences between inside hurts and outside hurts. It will teach us how Jesus is concerned about us when we hurt or suffer, especially if the hurt is inside.

MUST HAVES
- Adhesive bandage
- Paper bag
- 3x5 index cards
- Pencils

TO-DO LIST
- Gather or arrange to have tarps or paper for the children to sit on at the shop.
- Gather the materials for the object lesson.

SET!

There are several things to see at an auto body shop. Ask for a complete tour which would include the parking lot where the wrecked vehicles are brought, the office where the assessment of the damage is done,